RR (English Literature / History & Criticism)

ISSN 1350 4770

£6-
ART
03
13

D0470087

Women in European Theatre

Edited by Elizabeth Woodrough

1

WITHDRAWN FROM
THE LIBRARY

UNIVERSITY OF
WINCHESTER

EUROPA

KA 0227668 2

intellect

EUROPEAN STUDIES SERIES

General Editor: *Keith Cameron*

Humour and History	Edited by Keith Cameron
The Nation: Myth or Reality?	Edited by Keith Cameron
Regionalism in Europe	Edited by Peter Wagstaff
Women in European Theatre	Edited by Elizabeth Woodrough
Children and Propaganda	Judith Proud
The New Russia	Edited by Michael Pursglove
European Food	Edited by John Wilkins
Theatre and Europe 1957-1992	Christopher McCullough and Leslie du S Read
The European Community: Culture and Society	John Fletcher

Cover illustration:
L'Entree des comédiens dans la ville du Mans (Courtesy of the Museum of Le Mans)

First Published in 1995 by
Intellect Books
Suite 2, 108/110 London Road, Oxford OX3 9AW

Copyright ©1995 Intellect Ltd.

All rights reserved. No part of this publication may be reproduced, stored in a retrieval system, or transmitted, in any form or by any means, electronic, mechanical, photocopying, recording, or otherwise, without written permission.

British Library Cataloguing in Publication Data Available

ISBN 1-871516-86-2

Printed and bound in Great Britain by Cromwell Press, Wiltshire

CONTENTS

KING ALFRED'S COLLEGE
WINCHESTER

792
082
WOO   0227682

Introduction
Elizabeth Woodrough

Elizabeth Woodrough is Lecturer in the Department of French at the University of Exeter.

This collection of essays on the theme of European women players and playwrights arises from a one-day conference held in March 1993 at the Institute of Romance Studies at the University of London⋆. The intention was to set the achievements of Aphra Behn — arguably the first professional woman dramatist — in a wider context, and to take the theme as far afield and as far forward in time as one revolution of the sun would allow. Cutting across time and place, the essays move from the arrival of actresses on the English Restoration stage to political — and politicised — women's theatre in Italy in the sixties and seventies. They explore the situation of women working in the theatre as actresses, dramatists, and administrators; entering the cash economy through a literary domain which increased the social prejudice against them, even as it hastened the emancipation of their sex. Occasional theatrical triumphs are noted, as are the unpublished, unperformed, or poorly produced plays which women wrote and others directed. Whatever their successes and failures, many of the women concerned subsequently withdrew from the theatre altogether, taking refuge in silence, or safer genres.

By addressing the situation of female players and playwrights in successive papers, we are naturally drawn to consider the written playscript and the performance as of equal importance, avoiding the one-sided emphasis on the written text which has been identified as a problem area for women's theatre in search of a history.

The early essays bring together acting talents as diverse as those of Nell Gwyn, Elizabeth Barry, and Harriet Smithson in England, Mesdemoiselles Molière, Champmeslé, Du Parc, Adrienne Lecouvreur, Marie Dorval, and Sarah Bernhardt in France with, in Germany, Frau Neuber. The common theme here, not surprisingly, is the exploitation of the female form by male dramatists, and even by a number of the first of the women dramatists. Among those women writing for the theatre who emerge from the shadows in the later essays are Mme de Villedieu (France); Frau Gottsched, Berta Lask, Ilse Langner, and Marieluise Fleisse (Germany); G.B. Stern and Sylvia Rayman (England); Natalia Ginzburg, Dacia Maraini and Franca Rame (Italy).

When uncovering or rediscovering a body of forgotten, neglected or abandoned works by women, one must inevitably face the question of the quality of their output relative to the mainstream male playwrights. Should women simply have been content to have won acceptance as actresses and never gone on to write plays? It is a thankless task to set about recognising the natural inferiority of plays that usually had short runs if they were performed at all, and could not — and still cannot on the whole — hope to compete on equal grounds with the major successes of their day. Nor can one

⋆ I would like to express my gratitude to Simona Cain of the Institute for her assistance.

constantly be acclaiming the unsung work of women dramatists as unappreciated masterpieces, suppressed by jealous male rivals. It is partly the role of the academic in women's studies simply to make the fact more widely known that plays that may never have appeared in print were written against all the odds, and speak to us both directly and indirectly of the condition of a sex that might have been excluded altogether from the theatre. We cannot judge how future generations will view them, but we can help to make it possible for them to do so.

At a time when the domination of women in the area of gender studies in British and American universities is in itself the subject of polemic, it is important to acknowledge that the majority of contributors to this issue of *Europa* are again women, and that the audience for the conference was also mainly female. Plays that deal with women's issues, that describe, for instance, what it feels like to be a single mother, or tell tales of actresses required to jump off balconies onto the stage when eight months pregnant, will have special interest for women, particularly when they have experienced pregnancy or are pregnant, as was the case of two of the speakers at the conference. But sexual difference has not kept, and need not keep, men out of women's drama. Whether as mentors, producers or collaborators, men have assisted most of the women studied here; women who did not share the general preference of their sex for secret writing and the private or anonymous, but wished instead to become associated with the public domain of theatre. Nevertheless, far too many women in the theatre have, like Frau Gottsched in early eighteenth-century Germany, allowed their talents to serve the cause of a man's reputation.

The idea for a study of this kind arose from collaborative work on the *Bloomsbury Guide to Women's Literature* (ed. C. Buck). 'The first reference guide to the extraordinary riches of women's writing throughout the ages and throughout the world', this bio-bibliographical dictionary provides evidence of how many women have written novels and extensive correspondence, and of how few women of any nationality have even now actually written plays. The planning of the conference coincided with the publication of the late Lizzie Howe's ground-breaking book on Restoration actresses. It seemed fitting that we should dedicate our day to the memory of this young and talented academic. We were honoured by the presence of her husband, her supervisor and colleagues from the Open University where she was a Lecturer, and of her editor from Cambridge University Press. In publishing here Sarah Stanton's account of how Lizzie turned her research into a book, by way of an introduction to a previously unpublished paper by Lizzie herself on the sexuality of the Restoration theatre, it is hoped to draw attention to the situation of the woman academic today and to the conditions in which she works to refocus attitudes towards the creativity of her sex.

Jan Clarke's complementary study of women theatre professionals in seventeenth-century France explores the dichotomy of the actress as sinner and saint, without neglecting the more mundane duties of this sex 'in the box office, as usherettes, in the refreshment booths, and in the preparation of costumes and decors'. One of the most interesting questions she poses is why actresses, having become shareholders in theatrical companies, should have been apparently so ready to abandon the equal rights which they seemed to have won without even trying, and to abdicate their corporate administrative responsibility.

My own paper on the female dramatists of this period in France and England draws a parallel between Aphra Behn and Mme de Villedieu. A decade before the Great Astrea, her less famous contemporary briefly earned a living as a dramatist, collaborated with Molière, and enjoyed the double honour of being the first woman to have a play professionally performed in Paris and the first to receive a command performance at Versailles.

The male perspective in this volume is represented by Christopher Smith's paper on 'French Romanticism and the actresses', which takes us forward to the late eighteenth century and portrays the diverse talents of a bevy of beautiful actresses, famed in theatrical history for their uninhibited acting styles which were admirably suited to the portrayal of romantic durability. It is suggested that they had the paradoxical good fortune of not having their temperaments crushed by strict training, as happened to their male counterparts.

The next two papers on German women's theatre remind us how the best among them might from time to time be tolerated or patronised, without their work ever being very actively promoted, arousing considerable opposition the moment they began to stir the public imagination. Lesley Sharpe focuses on the early eighteenth century, so heavily influenced by French theatre, comparing the contribution of the first *Prinzipalin* (actress-manageress), Caroline Neuber, and Frau Gottsched, the mother of high German comedy. Both worked under the direction of Frau Gottsched's husband, Johann Christoph, a founding force in the new German theatre, whose assistance was a mixed blessing to the women whose cause he championed: Frau Neuber, an independent spirit, broke with her former ally, while Frau Gottsched had not the same freedom of movement and suffered in silence. Though conservative in tendency, her satirical comedies, which ridiculed the pretentions of the middle classes and the lower aristocracy, formed, along with her many translations from the French, the basis of a new comic repertoire in Germany.

Agnès Cardinal focuses on the social drama of three German women playwrights from the 1920s, who also gained little enough glory for their brave new work dramatising what war and deprivation can do to women. She reminds us that while collaboration with Brecht may have ensured that a female playwright like Marieluise Fleisser received at least some posthumous recognition, by his directorial interventions he could massacre her text. From a fascinating range of women's dramatic *oeuvres* after the First World War, one play stands out: Ilse Langner's *Frau Emma kämpft immer im Hinterland*, itself a possible model for Brecht's *Mother Courage*, for which Langner was pilloried as well as praised. Truncated, then kept off stage, *Frau Emma* is a play which gives a new twist to the theme of the working wife.

The final two papers between them span seven decades of women's theatre in the twentieth century and show women caught between the home, work and politics. In her survey of the London Stage from 1918 to 1968, Maggie Gale confronts the issue of feminist theatres head on by concentrating on the work of those who would normally be excluded from such a category. She uncovers a vast number of professionally produced plays, though there is no room for the notion of shared 'sisterhood' here. She brings two of the best among them to life. In the first, G.B. Stern's *The Man Who Plays the Piper*, the woman works, gives up work, feels bored and goes back to work, but cannot bring herself to accept the idea of a 'house-husband'. Sylvia Rayman's *Women of Twilight* is a surprisingly early kitchen-sink drama, which reflects on the plight of the single mother and may well be due for revival in the current political climate.

In what may appear a radical departure from the earlier papers, but is in some ways merely an extension of the concerns of Cardinal and Gale, Sharon Wood relates the dramatic aesthetics of three Italian women dramatists, none of whom first made their name by writing plays, to their own reflections on feminism and politics. She notes how Ginzberg, for instance, with her 'actorless' roles, refuses to work from the premise that all women are simultaneously oppressed and somehow superior, or to accept that writing or thought can be gendered. The novelist and director-manager, Maraini, who was the driving force behind the *Teatro della Maddelena*, a women's theatre workshop, is consistent in her plays, Wood argues, as well as in her feminism, politics, and sexual politics, however often she claims to put art before them. Wood's last example, the author-actress Franca Rame, is a living reminder of the dangers to which politically committed dramatists expose themselves. By her association with Dario Fo, Rame demonstrates that women do not have to write in isolation from male dramatists in order to be interesting.

Women dramatists such as these seem ready for the kind of exposure on the wider European stage that is only possible now that so many of the barriers are down. Where the essays that follow awaken echoes of women's voices that we have not explored here, we can only hope that others will extend this analysis of the multiformity of women's experience of drama.

Lizzie Howe   (Permission granted by Jeremy Howe)

Lizzie Howe: a dedication to her memory

Sarah Stanton

Sarah Stanton is Senior Commissioning Editor at Cambridge University Press

I should perhaps briefly explain my involvement with *The First English Actresses* and its author Elizabeth Howe, who died in 1992, only a few weeks after the book, her first, was published. Lizzie, as I came to know her, did not live to see the excellent reviews which have since appeared and which testified to the original nature of her research and its importance for the study of female acting and of playwriting during the forty years following the Restoration.

Early in 1989 Elizabeth Howe wrote to me asking whether CUP would publish a version of her PhD thesis on The Impact of the Actress on English Drama 1660-1700, for which she had first studied under Inga-Stina Ewbank, at what was then Bedford College. I took advice on the kind of changes that would be necessary to make the work publishable and Lizzie was later given a contract for publication.

Preparing the revised version was not a simple matter: Lizzie and I agreed that although the potential market was broad, because the subject matter had intrinsic popular appeal (everyone having heard of Nell Gwyn, and so on), the heavily-documented narrative required some leavening in order to attract non-specialists who had an interest in women on the stage, or, still more broadly and more vaguely, those in "women's studies".

The feminist appeal was inbuilt, but needed sharper focus and, on Lizzie's part, some further reading. One of the largest demands which I made on the author was the creation of a completely new first chapter on the workings of the Restoration theatre, in order to open up the subject for non-specialists and to give context to the ensuing analysis. This she did without a murmur, in a matter of weeks, and it is one of the most succinct and useful summaries on the market.

After months of correspondence came the only occasion on which we actually met, at Lizzie's house in Oxford, where I went to discuss some further small alterations and pictures for the book. It was then that I realised that here was no ordinary post-doctoral student. Lizzie had completed her PhD in Belfast with one small daughter at her side, and delivered the thesis, on time, just before she was delivered of her second baby daughter. She had taken the four-week old baby to London for her viva. Fortunately this was a fairly nominal affair, the examiners being more concerned by the howls of misery outside the room, emanating from little Lucy. I mention this partly to show the kind of determined and enormously efficient person that Lizzie was, and because the episode struck a chord in me, as it will in many who try to balance the ultimatums ('claims' is too weak a word) of family and professional life.

Lizzie was what I call a 'natural feminist'. She did not approach issues with a theory or method tucked into her belt, to be fired at all occasions; life had made her into a feminist, and a natural sense of justice and fairness made her support the disadvantaged, in whatever society they dwelt. Her work with the Open University, which she was proud to claim on the title-page of her book, was all of a piece with her strong social conscience. A shy, stammering, self-effacing person, she was a marvellous teacher and got very good results, not least from her students in the Maze Prison in Belfast.

The First English Actresses: Women and Drama 1660-1700 was published in May 1992. It is a study of what happened to English drama and theatre, playwriting and playing, as a result of the arrival of actresses onto the stage after the Restoration of Charles II. It is based on a thorough examination of every one of the surviving play texts from the period between 1660 and 1720; indeed, the first two years of Lizzie's research were spent in libraries reading texts. In addition, she read all the contemporary commentary by theatre critics and playgoers, visiting notables and diarists. The book is therefore written from both sides of the curtain, taking into account the play texts themselves, their all-important cast-lists, their prologues (spoken, as was the custom, by the actors and actresses), and such evidence as exists of the reception given to the plays, and theatre-going habits. It does not appear to have been written from a particular theoretical standpoint; it represents a process of discovery, based on hard evidence, which reaches sometimes uncomfortable conclusions. This is a piece of serious theatre history, whose subject matter and conclusions are carefully and elegantly directed towards a wide readership of historians, literary critics, and students of feminism.

Because the author had read so widely in the drama of the period, the book is, almost incidentally, a marvellous mine of information about the genres of Restoration comedy, melodrama and tragedy. There are brief plot summaries of the plays discussed. In many books about Restoration drama the only recurrent names are Dryden, Etherege, Wycherley, Vanbrugh, Congreve and Farquhar. Occasionally you may hear about plays by Otway and Southerne. Here the better-known plays, like Otway's *The Orphan*, are used as examples along with plays that are rarely discussed, to show (usually) how the female roles in these plays were created, extended, exploited, or made more or less interesting by the playwright as a result of the advent of certain actresses. Otway and Southerne feature here, along with the usual favourites, but John Crowne, Elkanah Settle, Nathaniel Lee, Nahum Tate, Thomas Durfey, Nicholas Rowe and many other writers are included. Of course, the plays by women playwrights of the period also included come under scrutiny: again, not only the better-known plays of Aphra Behn, such as *The Rover* (Hellena was an early vehicle for Elizabeth Barry), but those of the lesser-known writers, such as Delariviere Manley, Mary Pix, Susannah Centlivre and Catherine Trotter. Some of the plots may seem fairly trivial in themselves, but they become fascinating in this account because each new play is examined in the light of the particular cast that performed it, how it was devised for an occasion, or in the wake of a recent theatrical success, failure, or new acting partnership.

The book explores the characters and stage personalities of the various actresses, relatively few in number, who played at the time. After a discussion of the general increase in sex and violence, the almost gratuitous scenes of rape and prostitution which occurred on the stage during the 1660s and 1670s, the book shows how particular actresses became identified with certain roles, how audiences sometimes confounded the player with the part and how this type-casting, inherited from the Renaissance theatre, was then exploited by playwrights.

The detailed manner of the research enables the author to see new trends emerging; e.g., the introduction of 'she-tragedy' as a genre distinguished from heroic tragedy; the repetition from play to play of the so-called 'gay couple' of witty, bantering partners, beginning with Nell Gwyn and Charles Hart and reaching a climax in Dryden's *Secret Love,* in which they play Florimell and Celadon; the introduction of the 'lustful villainess' who seems to have been invented to exploit the special talents of Elizabeth Barry. In particular, we see the unfolding of a series of plays that are designed to use the complementary talents of, first, Elizabeth Boutell and Rebecca Marshall, and then Anne Bracegirdle and Elizabeth Barry, the 'angel' versus the 'she-devil'. We see how hard it was to break this mould, once the audience identified one woman as the virtous type and one as the whore.

Set against such developing patterns in the drama are the discoveries made about the lives, characters and careers of the women themselves. The heroine of the book turns out to be the highly versatile and accomplished 'darker woman', Elizabeth Barry. In her long career, Barry's acting, her ability to derive audience sympathy for the plight of the discarded or fallen woman, even for the woman driven to violent and criminal acts, seems to have inspired occasional playwrights to dispense with stereotypes and create real

Elizabeth Barry, after Godfrey Kneller
(By kind permission of the Garrick Club, E.T. Archive).

women. Barry played a range of roles; from young, vivacious girl, to prostitute, to elderly matron and passionate female villain. Her stage-presence was electric; her utterance of the simplest line of suffering caused stout hearts to melt.

Some of the book's conclusions are indeed pretty depressing. There is a relentless catalogue of scenes introduced into plays of the period apparently just to titillate male viewers, such as more-or-less explicit scenes of rape, the flaunting of female clothes in a state of disarray, bosoms revealed, semi-naked torsos. These all encouraged a prevailing perception, no doubt borne out by life itself, of the English actress as victim of male lust, as willing prostitute and as plaything for a prevailing male elite. None of the women had real power. Few became shareholders in their company, fewer still managers. The reader takes heart more by the contribution of individual actresses who raised the stakes of the drama of the time by their abilities, in tragedy and in comedy, and inspired the playwrights to create more interesting roles. The way in which playwright and player developed their skills hand-in-hand is evident in one sequence from Howe's book which shows the playwright Aphra Behn using and extending the acting talents and peculiar drawing power of the actress Elizabeth Barry.

Barry played the witty and provocative Hellena in Behn's *The Rover* (1677). In *The Second Part of The Rover* (1681) the role of the courtesan La Nuche is written for her; another interesting character. Although she plies a profitable career of prostitution, La Nuche finally abandons it in favour of a permanent alliance with her lover Willmore — not marriage, but a long, happy partnership in poverty. In *The City Heiress* (1682) Behn goes one step further and shifts the female focus of the play to the role of Lady Galliard, again played by Barry, who consummates her romantic attachment to the rake, Wilding, but forces herself to marry someone else, safely but without love, thus providing a realistic conclusion to the problem of a woman who gives herself to a libertine.

This sequence illustrates the great strength of Howe's book. She always shows Restoration theatre operating as a practical team effort in which the dramatist writes, for a familiar audience, a play that is to be performed by a particular company and by a well-known cast for whom he or she creates distinctive roles. Knowing audience expectations he or she treads a well-worn path; but knowing the actors' abilities, sensing their power over that audience, the playwright sometimes tries something astonishingly new and bold.

The First English Actresses tackles a popular subject, which, in some senses, could hardly fail to attract attention, given the twin focus on women and on a period of history associated, rightly or wrongly, with glamour, sex and people in high places (court culture). But the book's long-term value as a definitive work of reference is also assured. It offers a seamless conjunction of drama and theatre history, the text and who played it, how the lines were said as well as what they meant, by whom and to what effect.

A State of Undress. The first English actresses on stage: 1660-1700

Elizabeth Howe

Introduction
Inga-Stina Ewbank

Inga-Stina Ewbank is Professor of English Literature at the University of Leeds and was the supervisor of Elizabeth Howe's PhD thesis.

When Elizabeth Howe's life was cut short, her first book — The First English Actresses: Women and Drama 1660-1700 (C.U.P., 1992) — had just been published and she was deep into the research for her second book, which was to be about women and drama in the eighteenth century.

The paper printed here was given to the Women's Studies Group weekend conference on Liminality in History, in Fiction and on Stage *in June 1989 organised by Yvonne Noble and Elspeth Graham. It obviously antedates* The First English Actresses; *and, as Lizzie would have been the first to point out, most of the material is, in one form or another, included in that book. As she writes here, 'the actresses' dramatic role was not always and exclusively that of a sex object: in time leading female performers achieved a good deal more than this' — and the book explores 'a good deal more'. But the paper, structured for the occasion, conducts its own specific argument, demonstrating both economically and graphically how the Restoration theatre exploited the body of the actress, to produce what the author calls 'a new kind of stage rhetoric'.*

It seems appropriate that it should be published as part of the record of the workshop on Women Players and Playwrights *which was dedicated to her memory.*

1660 was a momentous year both for England and for English theatre. In 1660, the monarchy was restored, the public theatres reopened after a break of some eighteen years and a royal warrant was issued decreeing that in future women rather than boy actors would perform female roles on the public stage.[1]

The arrival of actresses in the public theatre did not mean the arrival of a new professional class of emancipated women in society. Society's preconceptions dictated that the arrival of actresses signified primarily the arrival of female bodies for public display. The first actresses were seen, above all, as objects — to be exploited for their beauty and for their sexual vulnerability. Their essential attributes were physical, not mental, and in this way they by and large confirmed, rather than challenged, the attitudes to gender in their society. The actresses' dramatic role was not always and exclusively that of a sex object: in time, leading female performers achieved a good deal more than this. However, in general, the women were perceived in terms of their physical attractions and exploited accordingly, with striking consequences for English drama. In

1. See A. Nicoll, *A History of English Drama 1660–1900*, Vol. I (Cambridge, 1955), p.304, n.3.

exploring some of these consequences I shall in a sense be exploring a new kind of stage rhetoric, both verbal and visual, made possible by the presence of women in the theatre, but conditioned by social assumptions and tastes.

From the beginning it was obvious that the new actresses and their physical attractions constituted for both the two London theatres a major means of pulling in the crowds, and by the 1670s comic dramatists began to capitalise on this in various ways. It is no coincidence, for instance, that it was this decade, the period in which the actresses had begun to prove their abilities and yet were still a comparative novelty, which saw a boom in so-called 'sex-comedy', a brand of comic drama focused on the efforts of a wife and lover to enjoy adultery without the husband's knowledge. Such comedy contained a striking degree of sexual explicitness in both language and action. The plays offered audiences alluring glimpses of female semi-nudity in a proliferation of bedroom scenes involving wives and their young lovers in a state of undress. For example, in Aphra Behn's *Sir Patient Fancy* of 1678, the act of adultery is presented with an unprecedented explicitness. In one scene, the erring wife, Lady Fancy, appears on the stage with her lover in a bedroom directly after lovemaking — she in a nightdress, he pulling on his clothes — while a few scenes later Lady Fancy is found again in the bedroom 'in disorder' as the stage direction puts it.[2] For this euphemism (never, incidentally, used as a stage direction like this, so far as I am aware, before 1660), we can assume from the dialogue and from contemporary illustrations that probably most, if not all, of the actress's bosom was exposed;[3] there could have been no possibility of using a boy here!

Similarly, for *The London Cuckolds* three years later, Edward Ravenscroft provided a bedroom scene which refers so precisely to the physical 'charms' of the woman involved as to have made the performance of a boy in the role of wife all but technically impossible. In one scene the wife's lover unexpectedly appears in her bedroom and announces that he is going to seduce her:

> Madam, come, your nightdress becomes you so well, and you look so very tempting — I can hardly forbear you a minute longer.

Having refused him in such a manner as to encourage him as much as possible the wife makes her exit, whereupon her maid assures the lover that 'she has nothing but her night-gown to slip off'.[4] There are a variety of similar scenes in comedy of the 1670s and 1680s.

Restoration adaptations of earlier comedies show very clearly how the opportunity for more explicit sex scenes was eagerly seized after 1660. Aphra Behn, who clearly had no qualms about exploiting her own sex, was particularly fond of inserting bedroom scenes and characters in an 'undress' into her adaptations of earlier dramas. For *The Debauchee, or, The Credulous Cuckold* of 1677,[5] for instance, she extended the original bedroom scene in Act III of her original, Brome's *A Mad Couple Well Match'd* (1637–9). While Brome merely gave the stage direction 'Bed put forth, Alicia in it', Behn demanded 'A Bed-Chamber, Alicia sitting in her Nightgown at a Table

2. A. Behn, *Sir Patient Fancy*. (London, 1678), pp.38, 63.

3. As J. H. Wilson has shown (*All the King's Ladies*, pp.68-71), Lady Fancy's nightdress would probably have been a loose, linen garment with a low drawstring neck, allowing a considerable degree of decolletage.

4. E. Ravenscroft, *The London Cuckolds* (London, 1682), pp.26-7.

5. The play's author is not definitely known, but is now usually assumed to be Aphra Behn. For a discussion of authorship, see H.A. Hargreaves, *The Life and Plays of Mrs Aphra Behn* (an unpublished PhD dissertation), (Duke University, 1960).

undressing her'. At the end of the scene she has one of the men take Alicia to bed while Brome could only symbolise a coupling with the cryptic stage direction 'puts in the bed'.[6]

A similar alteration was made to Middleton's *No Wit No Help Like a Woman's* (c.1617) in *The Counterfeit Bridegroom* (1677), again probably by Aphra Behn.[7] The final act of the later version offers, 'Widow discover'd sittinq on a Bed, in a Nightgown, Noble in Bed holding her by the Gown'. Noble tries to rape the widow, they struggle and she breaks free. In the equivalent scene in Middleton's play, the couple simply 'enter confusedly' after the door to the bedroom is broken down.

At the same time as they made the sexual action of such plays more explicit, dramatists of the 1670s and after also tended to give a new kind of detailed description of their female characters' appearance, again dwelling particularly on their breasts, in order to draw attention to the body of the actress in question. In *The Careless Lovers* (1673) by Ravenscroft, for example, one of the heroes points out the attractions of the heroine's figure:

A handsome Legg and Foot I'le be sworn; and here's a well shap'd Hand and Arme; and what Breasts are here? How round and plump?

In Thomas Shadwell's *A True Widow* (1678), the elderly Lady Busy attempts to persuade a young man to marry her daughter by giving him a catalogue of the girl's physical assets:

Ah what pleasure 'tis to lye by such a sweet Bedfellow! such pretty little swelling Breasts! such delicate black sparkling eyes! such a fresh Complexion! such red powting Lips! and such a Skin! [8]

In addressing her daughter in this way, Lady Busy is in a sense also putting the actress's body on display for the benefit of spectators — a new kind of stage rhetoric. Such descriptions probably mirrored the actual actresses who took the roles; certainly the picture of Florimell in Dryden's *Secret Love* (1667), 'such an Ovall Face, clear skin, hazel eyes, thick brown Eye-browes and Hair',[9] we know from portraits to be a description of Nell Gwyn, who played Florimell.

One consequence of the arrival of actresses then seems to have been that in drama about sexual relations between men and women a new correlation was possible, and indeed emphasised, between erotic, explicit language about female characters and the appearance of the players acting those characters on the stage — a correlation which was naturally not possible with boy actors. In literature before 1660, therefore, one finds necessarily a split between dramatic and non-dramatic representations of women as sexual objects. Renaissance poets could, and did, write as explicitly and as erotically as Restoration ones. For instance, the tradition of the erotic epyllion to which Shakespeare's *Venus and Adonis* belongs is carried to its extreme in Marston's *The Metamorphosis of Pigmalion's Image* (1598). But there is no comparable degree of directly physical language in Renaissance drama. Even Cleopatra, surely the most sexual of Shakespeare's heroines, is never described physically. Typically, the famous account of Cleopatra in her barge, given to Agrippa by

6. R. Brome, *A Mad Couple Well Match'd* (London, 1653), IV, iii. A. Behn, *The Debauchee* (London, 1677), p.47.

7. See Hargreaves, *The Life and Plays of Mrs. Aphra Behn*. pp.260-71.

8. E. Ravenscroft, *The Careless Lovers* (London, 1673), p.9. T. Shadwell, *A True Widow* (London, 1679), p.61.

9. J. Dryden, *Works of John Dryden*, general editor H.T. Swedenberg Jr. (Berkeley and Los Angeles, 1954–1993), Vol. IX, *Secret Love*, I, ii, pp.48-9.

Enobarbus,[10] is a marvellous account of the objects around the queen, but offers no physical detail about the woman herself. There is much less difference then between the erotic language in Rochester's poems — say — and that spoken (and manifested) on stage at the time than there is between the descriptions of passion in *Venus and Adonis* and the spoken passion of hero and heroine in *Antony and Cleopatra*.

The intent to use the language of drama to deliberately point up the sexual attraction and femininity of the actress is as marked in Restoration tragedy as it is in comedy. The first part known to have been taken by a woman in a tragedy on the public stage was Desdemona in a 1660 revival of Shakespeare's *Othello*. Restoration productions seem to have intensified the eroticism of the play with a good deal of visual sensuality. In her preface to *The Dutch Lover* (1673), Aphra Behn defended what had been attacked as prurient elements in her drama by citing various pre-Restoration plays with a similar element, and she included among these, 'The Moor of Venice in many places'.[11] The frontispiece illustration to *Othello* in Nicholas Rowe's 1709 edition of the works of Shakespeare shows a bare-breasted Desdemona sprawled across a bed, Othello moving towards her with a pillow, and this picture probably illustrates actual stage practice. The mental traits which make Desdemona a strong character and an individual were probably of less interest to Restoration audiences and dramatists.

Frontispiece engraving to Othello (Courtesy of the Bodleian Library)

Prevailing modes of tragedy, like those of comedy, were adapted and modified from 1660 to include more sensual descriptions, more erotic love scenes, more rape and the introduction of what I would call 'couch scenes'. A strikingly popular dramatic device developed in the placing of the actress on the stage asleep on a couch, bed or grassy bank where, attractively defenceless and frequently half undressed, she offered a sexual thrill to the audience while, in the play, unwittingly arousing desire in the male viewing her.

For example, In John Crowne's *The History of Charles the Eighth of France, or, The Invasion of Naples by the French* (1671), Charles gazes with desire upon the sleeping heroine Julia as this song is sung:

> Yet Oh Ye Powers! I'd dye to gain
> But one poor parting Kiss!
> And yet I'de be on Wracks of pain, '
> 'Ere I'de one Thought or Wish retain,
> Which Honour thinks amiss.[12]

Later in the same play, Julia's companions, Cornelia and Irene, offer another picture of unconscious femininity, 'presented asleep upon a couch! and at their feet Sylvia'.[13] In a later play, Thomas Southerne's

10. Shakespeare, *Complete Works* (ed. P. Alexander), (London & Glasgow, 1951), *Antony and Cleopatra*, II, ii, 195–209.
11. A. Behn, *The Luckey Chance or The Alderman's Bargain* (London, 1687), preface.
12. J. Crowne, *The History of Charles the Eighth of France*: (London, 1672), p.47.
13. Ibid., p.68.

14. T. Southerne, *The Works of Thomas Southerne*, ed. Robert Jordan and Harold Love (Oxford, 1988), Vol. II, *The Fate of Capua*, III, v 13-8.

15. For a full account of rape in these plays, see S. Gossett, '*Best Men and Molded out of Faults*: Marrying the Rapist in Jacobean Drama', *English Literary Renaissance*, 14 (1984), pp. 305-27.

16. Dryden criticised the female characters of Fletcher. 'Let us applaud his scenes of love; but let us confess, that he understood not either greatness or perfect honour in the parts of any of his women.' See *Essays of John Dryden*, ed. W. P. Ker (Oxford, 1900), Vol. I, p. 177.

The Fate of Capua (1700), a wife, Favonia, is seen 'asleep on a Couch in an undress' while her husband's friend Junius stares hungrily:

— let me fix here —
Stretch wide the Gates of sight to take her in,
In the full triumph of her conquering charms.
My eager Eyes devour her Beauties up,
Insatiable, and hungring still for more.
O! the rich Glutton, that enjoys this store! [14]

This idea of sleeping female beauty being watched lustfully by a possibly dangerous male was not new: in Shakespeare's *Cymbeline*, Iachimo has a whole scene in which to gaze on the sleeping Imogen, having previously gained access to her bedroom. However, a comparison of the speech above, inspired by the half-naked Favonia, and Iachimo's words as he looks at Imogen, illustrates how much more overtly erotic the device became with a real woman on the stage. It is significant that Iachimo's most sensual lines about his experience — his account of kissing the mole beneath Imogen's breast — are spoken afterwards to Posthumus, and that he is lying. The erotic image here is an imaginary one. It is only in the Restoration tragedy that male lust is directly aroused by a visual female image.

The most striking sexual consequence of the use of actresses in tragedy is the number of rapes it produced in the genre. The introduction of actresses caused rape to become for the first time a major feature of English tragedy. From 1594 to 1612, for instance, there are only four plays in which rape actually occurs and there are only five between 1612 and 1625.[15] After 1660, in just over 40 years, I have found no less than 37 plays in which rapes or near rapes occur. Rapes were, of course, a dramatic means of giving the purest, most virginal heroine a sexual quality. They allowed dramatists to create women of such 'greatness' and 'perfect honour'[16] as was felt to be appropriate to tragedy and heroic drama, but at the same time to exploit sexually the new female presence in the theatre.

A rape could in fact allow a serious play to offer at least as good a display of naked female flesh as any sex-comedy. The high point of Dryden's *Amboyna, or, The Cruelties of the Dutch* (1673), for instance, is the rape of the heroine which takes place only just off stage. Ysabinda is dragged pleading from the audience's view, her seducer reappearing shortly afterwards to relate the rape for the audience's benefit. The scene, or painted flat, is then drawn to reveal the unfortunate Ysabinda in some disarray and

Frontispiece engraving to Amboyna
(Courtesy of the Bodleian Library)

bound. An illustration to the 1735 *Collected Works of Dryden*, which could have been taken from an actual stage production, implies that a good deal of her body was exposed in this scene. Her bosom was presumably displayed since her lover comments as he unties her, 'Your Breast is white, and cold as falling snow'.[17]

As the device came to be used more frequently, the rape had to be described more and more explicitly to satisfy an audience which had heard so many such descriptions before. Thus by 1696 Mary Pix's *Ibrahim, The Thirteenth Emperour of the Turks* offers first of all the build-up to the rape as Ibrahim marches off-stage with the resolution, 'I'll rush thro' all and seize the trembling prey', then the appearance of the victim, 'her Hair down and much disorder'd in her dress', and finally an explicit account of the experience related by her father to her lover:

> — suppose
> Her prayers, her tears, her cryes,
> Her wounding supplications all in vain,
> Her dear hands in the Conflict cut and mangled,
> Dying her white Arms in Crimson Gore,
> The savage Ravisher twisting his hands (sic)
> In the lovely Tresses of her hair,
> Tearing it by the smarting Root,
> Fixing her, by that upon the ground:
> Then — (horrour on horrour!)
> On her breathless body perpetrate the fact.[18]

To illustrate this account, 'The Scene draws and discovers Morena upon the ground disorder'd as before'. As frequently occurred, the novelty of moving 'scenes', or flats, is here combined with the female body in order to provide a thrilling spectacle. Having expressed her wretchedness and raised her bloody hands for justice the scene shuts upon Morena. This use of the moving scene emphasises the way in which Restoration theatre offered the body of the actress to the audience as a piece of erotic entertainment, a kind of pornographic painting brought to life.

The insistent physicality of Restoration presentations of rape makes a striking contrast with Shakespeare's handling of Lavinia's rape in *Titus Andronicus*. Here the audience is acutely aware as they watch the play that the violation is taking place off stage and Lavinia must presumably have reappeared in an appropriate state of dishevelment, and with wounds to signify that her hand, and tongue, have been cut off. However, the language which her father Titus uses in the face of her suffering, with its classical references and self-conscious word-play, distances us from the physical actuality of her pain and anguish:

> Speak Lavinia, what accursed hand
> Hath made thee handless in thy father's sight?
> What fool hath added water to the sea,
> Or brought a fagot to bright-burning Troy?
> [...]Tis well, Lavinia, that thou hast no hands;
> For hands to do Rome service is but vain.

17. J. Dryden, *Amboyna* (London, 1673), p.45.
18. M. Pix, *Ibrahim, The Thirteenth Emperour of the Turks*: (London, 1696), p.2.

Likewise the speech of Lavinia's uncle Marcus transforms the hideous reality of Lavinia's tongue being cut out into a beautiful image:

> Why dost not speak to me?
> Alas, a crimson river of warm blood,
> Like to a bubbling fountain stirr'd with wind,
> Doth rise and fall between thy rosed lips,
> Coming and going with thy honey breath.
> But sure some Tereus hath deflowered thee,
> And, lest thou shouldst detect him, cut thy tongue.[19]

This poetry seems, in a way, divorced from Lavinia's physical condition: it creates an imagistic world of its own and so reduces much of our sense of her maiming. By contrast, with the arrival of women actresses, in plays such as Dryden's *Amboyna* and Pix's *Ibrahim*, spectacle and speech support one another, and what the characters speak is used to elicit a response to what spectators can see. In engendering a new correlation on the stage between action and rhetoric, the actress helped to break down what, in Renaissance theatre, had been a necessary dislocation between the visual and the verbal, a dislocation which kept the physical reality of heterosexual sex for ever at a distance, even in the most bawdy of dramas.

The sexual exploitation of the new actresses has a significance which goes beyond changes to the nature of drama. The fact that the actresses were utilised primarily as sexual objects suggests something about the Restoration age in general; although in this society women were permitted to perform alongside men on the public stage, paradoxically this licence often merely served to underline female limitations. A few women gained entry into a hitherto male-dominated profession, but as they pursued it, they largely reinforced traditional female stereotypes on the stage. Thus the social status quo seems not to have been seriously threatened by the arrival of the actress: in the small, controlled environment of a coterie theatre she usually performed in a manner which upheld dominant attitudes to gender.

19. Shakespeare, *Titus Andronicus*: III, i, 66-69, 79-80. II, iv, 21-27. For an account of the split between language and action in *Titus Andronicus*, see E. Waith, 'The Metamorphosis of Violence' in *Titus Andronicus*', *Shakespeare Survey*: 10, (Cambridge, 1957), pp.39-49.

Women Theatre Professionals in 17th-century France
Jan Clarke

Jan Clarke is Lecturer in French in the Department of Modern Languages at Keele University.

This article is divided into three sections. First, I examine contemporary attitudes to actresses in seventeenth-century France, with particular reference to methods proposed to limit the potential danger of the sexual attraction they exerted. Next, I consider the views of certain critics up to the middle of the twentieth century. This section could be subtitled: 'The actress as source of all evils — the case of Mlle Molière'. Finally I attempt to suggest some new approaches and unexplored areas — particularly that of the role played by women in theatre administration.

Inevitably, the history of the French theatre in the seventeenth century has been written by men. Almost all documents and original source materials were produced by men, since they occupied positions of authority in theatre administration and were charged with keeping records. Similarly, the vast majority of contemporary authors and social commentators were men, and, what is more, up until the second half of the twentieth century, the scholars who interpreted these various documents were almost always men. It is perhaps only a slight oversimplification to say that, in the main, whenever women (or at least actresses) appear in the accounts of either contemporary or subsequent commentators, it is in one of two stereotypical guises: either the actress as sinner or the actress as saint. First, let us consider the representation of the actress as sinner, as she appears in the accounts of certain of her contemporaries, and then in those of more recent critics.

The actress as sinner is probably the most conventional figure in the history of the theatre, typified in the popular view of Charles II's mistress Nell Gwynn. One of the main criticisms levelled at the public theatre in France in the seventeenth century concerned the morality of its actresses. There are innumerable reports of the disruption caused by the hordes of followers they attracted backstage, together with expressions of real or mock outrage at the apparent fashion for members of the Court to take actresses and opera singers as their mistresses.[1] This trend was led by the Dauphin, whose mistress, the Comédie-Française actress Mlle Raisin, can be compared to Nell Gwynn, not least in that she bore him a child.[2]

Frequently in this context we can see evidence of a dual standard in operation. One of the chief delights of the theatre was seen to reside in the attractiveness of its actresses, yet when they did attract they were criticised for arousing impure thoughts in the minds of male spectators. Such criticism was particularly virulent in the last years of the reign of Louis XIV, when religious revivalism had taken

1. See Mme du Noyer, *Lettres historiques et galantes*, Vol. I, 15 (letter II): in P. Mélèse, *Le Théâtre et le public à Paris sous Louis XIV (1659-1715)*, (Paris, Droz, 1934), p.176.
2. Mélèse, *Théâtre et public*, p.174.

KING ALFRED'S COLLEGE LIBRARY

a grip on almost all sections of society. For many commentators at this time, all actresses were sinning against the natural modesty of their sex merely by appearing and speaking in public. It was apparently still worse if they were married, for by desiring to appear beautiful in the eyes of male spectators, they were, in the view of their critics, automatically responsible, and therefore guilty in the eyes of God, for the sinful and thus adulterous thoughts they inspired.[3]

According to Du Tralage, the consequences of this attraction were inevitable if male members of the audience were allowed to sit in close proximity to the actresses. He wrote in 1696:

> *Autrefois on ne voulait point de femmes mariées à l'Opéra, maintenant il y en a trois avec leurs marys [...] La plupart des autres filles ont des patrons qui les entretiennent à grands frais; ce sont des femmes non mariées. Il y en a ordinairement quelqu'une incommodée du mal de ceinture, et dont il faut élargir le corps. Il n'y a guère d'années où cet accident n'arrive. Autrefois M. Lully n'entendoit pas de raillerie là-dessus, et personne n'alloit dans l'orchestre ny sur le théâtre, il n'y avoit que les acteurs et les musiciens; on s'est relâché par l'avidité du gain [...] C'est là que commencent toutes les amourettes et que se donnent les rendez-vous [...]*

> (In the past married women were not allowed to perform at the Opera, but now there are three there with their husbands [...] Most of the other girls have patrons who maintain them at great expense. These are unmarried women. There is ordinarily at least one of them inconvenienced by a pain in the belly, and whose bodice has to be let out. There are very few years when this accident does not occur. In the past M. Lully could not take a joke on the subject, and no one was allowed in the orchestra pit or on the stage apart from the actors and musicians, but this rule has been relaxed through greed.[...] It is there that all the adventures begin and where meetings are arranged [...])[4]

It is interesting that Du Tralage notes that previously only unmarried women had been allowed to perform at the Opera. This is unlikely to have been out of repugnance at the mass mental adultery previously described. It is more probable that it was because married women were deemed more likely to give in to their admirers, since any resulting pregnancy could be passed off as their husband's. Or else because married women were indeed frequently pregnant, and a pregnant actress was considered unattractive and therefore damaging to the stage spectacle. This was certainly the view of the Abbé de Pure, who in 1668 made the following suggestion:

> *Il serait à souhaiter que toutes les comédiennes fussent et jeunes et belles, et, s'il se pouvait, toujours filles, ou du moins jamais grosses. Car, outre que la fécondité de leur ventre coûte à la beauté de leur visage ou de leur taille, c'est un mal qui dure plus depuis qu'il a commencé qu'il ne tarde à revenir depuis qu'il a fini.*

> (It is to be wished that all actresses will be young and beautiful, and if possible all unmarried, or at least never pregnant. Because apart from the fact that the fertility of the belly destroys the beauty of the face and figure,

3. See J.H. Phillips, *The Theatre and its Critics in Seventeenth-Century France* (Oxford: Oxford University Press, 1980), pp.187-88.

4. J.-N. Du Tralage, *Recueil*, Vol. IV (1696), in Mélèse, *Théâtre et public*, pp.175-76.

it is an evil which lasts longer once it has begun than it takes to reappear once it is over.)[5]

On the other hand, D'Aubignac in *La Pratique du Théâtre* maintains that the association of the theatre with loose morals would be cured by employing only married women or unmarried women under strict control.

> *Et pour y conserver la bien-séance, ne pourront les filles monter sur le Theatre, si elles n'ont leur pere ou leur mere dans la Compagnie. Que les veuves seront obligées de se remarier dans les six mois d'après l'an de leur deüil au plus tard, et ne joueront point dans l'an de deüil, sinon qu'elles fussent remariées.*

> (To preserve the proprieties, unmarried women will only be allowed to go on the stage if they have their father or mother in the company. Widows will be obliged to remarry in the six months following their year of mourning at the latest, and will not be allowed to perform during their year of mourning unless they have remarried.)[6]

It is clear that here the male members of the audience are seen as being at risk from the uncontrolled sex-drive of unsatisfied, sexually experienced women. This gives a potentially interesting slant to Du Tralage's comment on the dangers of the proximity of actresses and male members of the audience on the stage.

But the fact that attentions by members of the audience *were* frequently unwelcome is occasionally demonstrated by contemporary documents. Thus Georges Forestier has shown how certain 'comédies des comédiens' feature this new type of 'fâcheux'.[7] Also of interest is an incident involving Mlle Molière. An admirer, who had fallen in love with the actress from afar, was tricked by a procuress into having an affair with a prostitute remarkably like her. Although under strict instructions never to speak to the actress in the theatre, he was one day unable to contain himself and persisted in making signs and whispering sweet nothings to her from the stage benches. When Mlle Molière did not respond, he burst into her dressing room, tore a necklace from her throat, and accused her of mistreating him. She was forced to have him evicted by the theatre guards, and finally gained legal satisfaction when the procuress and the prostitute were sentenced to be whipped in the street outside her house.[8]

Contemporary commentators do not only reveal a dual standard in relation to the attractiveness of actresses. A further, perhaps more common one, is displayed by the fact that whereas much is made of the supposedly loose morals of actresses, comparatively little is said of the behaviour of actors, unless it is that they connive in the immorality of the female company members and share all the available women between them. For example, Du Tralage writes that La Thorillière *fils* was paid by his friends to persuade his sister, Dancourt's wife, to sleep with them.[9] And Tallemant des Réaux goes even further, claiming that actors' wives

> *vivoient dans la plus grande licence du monde; c'étoient des femmes communes, même aux comédiens de la troupe dont elles n'étoient pas.*

5. *Idée des spectacles* (1668), in E. Despois, *Le Théâtre français sous Louis XIV* (Paris: Hachette, 1886), p.217.
6. F.H. d'Aubignac, *La Pratique du théâtre* (1715), ed. by H.J. Neuschäfer (Geneva: Slatkine, 1971), p.354.
7. 'L'Actrice et le fâcheux dans les "comédies des comédiens" du XVIIe siècle', *Revue d'histoire littéraire de la France*, Vol. LXXX (1980), pp.355-65.
8. See *La Fameuse comédienne* (1688), ed. by J. Bonnassies (Paris: Barraud, 1870).
9. J.-N. Du Tralage, *Notes et documents sur l'histoire des théâtres de Paris au XVIIe siècle* (1693) (Geneva: Slatkine, 1969).

lived with the greatest licence in the world, and were women used by the whole company, and even by actors in different troupes.)[10]

This last view is acknowledged and refuted by Scudéry in *La Comédie des comédiens*, who places the following speech in the mouth of the actress La Beausoleil:

ils pensent que la farce est l'image de nostre vie, & que nous ne faisons que representer ce que nous pratiquons en effect. Ils croient que la femme d'un de vous autres, l'est indubitablement de toute la Troupe; & s'imaginant que nous sommes un bien commun, comme le Soleil ou les Elemens, il ne s'en treuve pas un, qui ne croye avoir droict de nous faire souffrir l'importunité de ses demandes..

(They think that the farce is the image of our lives and that we only act out on stage what we practice in real life. They believe that the wife of any one of [the actors] unquestionably belongs to the whole troupe; and, imagining that we are communal property, like the sun or the elements, there is not one of them who does not believe he has the right to make us suffer the importunity of his demands.)[11]

This inability to distinguish the actress from her role is a question I will return to later.

I would like now to make a few general points regarding the representation of seventeenth-century actresses by scholars of the nineteenth and early twentieth centuries. While the majority of these worthy individuals acknowledge that actresses acted as a valuable source of inspiration for many dramatists, they also have a tendency to present women as sirens luring their conquests to spiritual or even actual destruction. Thus, it is frequently alleged that Mlle Molière's infidelity contributed in no small way to her husband's death. Loiseleur, for example, describes her as:

Cette femme d'esprit médiocre et de coeur nul, qui abreuva d'amertumes l'homme illustre dont la destinée était unie à la sienne, et qui, à la fin, abrégea ses jours.

(That woman of mediocre wit and no heart, who filled with bitterness the days of the illustrious man whose destiny was allied with hers, and finally cut them short.)[12]

Such an attitude could, of course, be seen merely as the product of a general misogyny, bearing little relation to Mlle Molière's profession. This view is contradicted, though, by Loiseleur's subsequent comment that it would have been more surprising if she had behaved

Mlle Champmeslé

10. T. des Réaux, *Les Historiettes*, ed. by Monmerqué, De Chateaugiron and Taschereau: 6 vols (1834-35), Vol. VI, p.11.

11. G. de Scudéry, *La Comédie des comédiens*, ed. by J. Crow (Exeter: University of Exeter, 1975), p.11.

12. J. Loiseleur, *Les Points obscurs de la vie de Molière* (Paris: Isidore Liseux, 1877), p.296.

in any other way, since the misconduct of actresses, like that of Jews in the Middle Ages, was an inevitable reaction to their ostracisation by society.[13]

Truly, though, the actress cannot win, for even those critics who acknowledge that Molière and his wife were reconciled shortly before the dramatist's death still find the means to lay the blame at her door, saying that it was on her account he gave up his strict diet. Thus, the English critic H. Noel Williams asserts categorically, 'The reconciliation with his wife, [...] in itself so happy, was destined to prove fatal to Molière, and was undoubtedly one of the causes of his premature death'.[14] Similarly, although on a lesser level of seriousness, the Parfaict brothers lay the blame for Racine's abandonment of the professional stage squarely on Mlle Champmeslé's infidelity.[15]

Even when matters are not so extreme, women are presented as being difficult to handle and greatly adding to the problems of company administration; although, in fairness, this is merely a reflection of a view frequently expressed by contemporary commentators.

Thus, La Chappelle's letter to Molière sympathising with his difficulty in allocating roles to please his three leading actresses is frequently quoted,[16] as are Chappuzeau's comments in *Le Théâtre français* that all actresses like to seem young, refuse to play mothers with children of an age to make them appear over forty, and in general are far more difficult to handle than men.[17] This may well be one explanation of the custom by which all elderly female parts were played by men.

But as for women being difficult to manage, whereas we have numerous accounts of actors actually coming to blows in the green-room and elsewhere, only comparatively rarely are there reports of disagreements between actresses. Moreover, the authenticity of such reports is sometimes open to question. For example, Dauvilliers and Mlle Dupin and their respective spouses were all expelled from the Guénégaud company for refusing to consent to the production of Thomas Corneille's machine play *Circé*. Their expulsion is, however, frequently presented as a consequence of Mlle Molière's jealousy of Mlle Dupin.[18]

Like their predecessors, nineteenth-century and early twentieth-century commentators also frequently found it difficult to dissociate the actress from her role. Thus, Mlle Molière is almost invariably identified with the parts written for her by her husband. Many also seem to have shared the view of contemporary critics that tragedy was the most elevated and dignified theatrical form. This created problems when they came to discuss the careers of tragediennes, for they often found it hard to reconcile this nobility with the lifestyle of, say, Mlle Champmeslé or Mlle Du Parc. There is dual standard in operation here too, though, and many critics at the same time display a prurient interest in the seamier side of theatrical life. Few, for example, can resist the temptation provided to quote the following description of Mlle Du Parc's provincial debut as an exotic dancer:

13. Ibid., p.302.
14. *Queens of the French Stage* (London and New York: Harper, 1905), p.60.
15. C. and F. Parfaict, *Histoire du théâtre français*, 14 vols (1734-49), 3 vols (Geneva: Slatkine, 1969), III, p.529.
16. R. Bray, *Molière homme de théâtre* (Mayenne: Mercure de France, 1954).
17. S. Chappuzeau, *Le Théâtre français* (1674), (Plan de la Tour: Editions d'aujourd'hui, 1985), p.75.
18. T. Corneille, *Circé*, ed. by Jan Clarke (Exeter: University of Exeter, 1989), pp. xxix-xxx.

on voyait ses jambes et partie de ses cuisses au moyen de sa jupe fendue des
deux côtés, avec des bas de soie, attachés au haut d'une petite culotte.

(her legs and part of her thighs could be seen since she wore a skirt split at
either side, and silk stockings attached to the top of a short pair of
drawers.)[19]

Above all, these critics cannot resist the temptation to sit in
judgement on the actresses they evoke. The main target of their
vitriol is inevitably Mlle Molière, who is criticised for her alleged
infidelity during her marriage to the playwright, for having returned
to the stage shortly after his death, and for having married her fellow
actor Guérin d'Estriché instead of remaining in some kind of purdah
as befitted the widow of so great a man. As a contemporary epigram
put it:

Elle avoit un mari d'esprit qu'elle aimoit peu;
Elle en prend un de chair qu'elle aime davantage.

(She had a husband of wit whom she loved little;
Now she has one of flesh whom she loves more.)[20]

If the supposedly questionable morality of actresses was one of the
chief weapons used by contemporary critics to attack the theatre, it
is not surprising that theatre-lovers should have leapt to their defence.
Some of these were, however, a little over-zealous, giving rise to
what one might call with only a slight exaggeration, the
phenomenon of the 'actress as saint'. Foremost amongst this group
is Chappuzeau, who writes (p. 75) of actors in general as follows:

Quoique la profession des comédiens les oblige de représenter incessamment
des intrigues d'amour, de rire et de folastrer sur le théâtre, de retour chez
eux ce ne sont plus les mêmes; c'est un grand sérieux et un entretien
solide; et dans la conduite de leurs familles on découvre la même vertu et la
même honnesteté que dans les familles des autres bourgeois qui vivent bien.

(Although the actor's profession obliges them ceaselessly to perform love
stories, to laugh and behave foolishly on the stage, once at home they are
completely different; their behaviour is serious and sound, and in their
conduct of family life we find the same virtue and upright behaviour as in
that of any other right-living bourgeois family.)

Other defenders of actresses, and thereby the theatre in general,
include those authors of *'comédies des comédiens'* who, as we have
seen, recognise the existence of hangers-on backstage, but who show
actresses resolutely preserving their virtue by invariably repulsing
their importunate admirers.

The representations of women I have outlined so far are clearly
very limited, not least in that female theatre professionals are seen
to consist almost exclusively of actresses. The balance has, though,
been redressed somewhat in the last fifty years, particularly through
the work of theatre historians such as S. Wilma Deierkauf-Holsboer
and Sylvie Chevalley. Many women other than actresses, singers
and dancers worked in the theatre. They were employed in the box-

19. K. Mantzius, *Molière: les*
théâtres, le public et les
comédiens de son temps
(Paris: Armand Colin,
1908), p. 73.
20. Loiseleur, *Points obscurs,*
pp. 367-69.

office, as usherettes, in the refreshment booths, and in the preparation of costumes and decors, in some cases occupying positions of responsibility over considerable periods of time.[21] For example, Mme Provost was in charge of the box-office both for Molière's troupe and at the Guénégaud theatre, and Mlle Michel and Mlle LaVillette ran the refreshments booths at the Guénégaud.[22] These were not, though, the only areas in which women worked. The seventeenth-century theatre was very much a family concern, with husbands and wives and sometimes children all working alongside each other, and frequently assisting each other in their duties, however physically arduous. Thus, figures who appear regularly in the Guénégaud company account books are not so much the leading ladies of the troupe, as Mme Dufors, the wife of the concierge, and Mme Crosnier, the wife of the *décorateur*. It was also frequently the case that retired actresses would move into front-of-house work. For example, Mlle Hubert was assistant to Mme Provost at the Guénégaud, and Mlle Guyot took over from Mme Provost at the Comédie-Française, where she was so attached to the company that she made its members her heirs.[23]

One of the most interesting of the neglected aspects of women's involvement in seventeenth-century theatre is the part they played in theatre administration. This was, in theory, equal to that played by men, for in Chappuzeau's words (p. 82):

L'authorité de l'Estat est partagée entre les deux sexes, les femmes luy estant utiles autant ou plus que les hommes, et elles ont voix délibérative en toutes les affaires qui regardent l'intérest commun.

(The authority of the State is divided between the two sexes, women being as useful or even more useful than the men; and they have a voice in all discussions regarding company affairs).

The importance attached to a person's utterances supposedly depended not on their gender but on the size of their share in the company, which could range from a full share to a quarter share, and which was awarded according to acting ability. The system was, though, subject to abuses both from outside and inside the company. Thus, at one point, an actress was imposed on the Guénégaud troupe against its will, and at another La Grange was obliged to defend his wife's right to a share in the same company.[24]

Chappuzeau's *Le Théâtre français* was published in 1674, describing the Parisian theatrical set-up as it had existed for fifty years or more. Things were changing, though, particularly with regard to women's involvement in company affairs, and a few key dates enable us to trace this evolution. In 1658, Madeleine Béjart took out a lease on the Marais theatre with a view to arranging the return of Molière's troupe to the capital. This, together with her control of the company's finances, is a clear indication of the major administrative role she played with the troupe.[25] In 1674, Chappuzeau recorded with some regret that women 'out of modesty' only rarely attended play selection meetings, even though they had the right to take an active part in all meetings (p. 56). Finally, in 1683, a decision was taken to

21. I have excluded women playwrights from this study on the grounds that since few depended on their theatre work for their livelihood most were not strictly professional.
22. S. Chevalley, 'Le "Registre d'Hubert" 1672-1673: étude critique', *Revue d'Histoire du Théâtre*, Vol. XXV (1973) 145-195 (pp. 192-93): Archives de la Comédie-Française, account books of the Guénégaud troupe.
23. Archives Nationales, Minutier Central, XLIV, p.113.
24. G. Monval, 'L'Affaire Auzillon', *Le Moliériste*, Vol. VIII (May-June 1868), pp.53-59, 73-85.
25. S. W. Deierkauf-Holsboer, *Le Théâtre du Marais*, 2 vols (Paris: Nizet, 1954-8), Vol. II, 95-97: E. Gaboriau, *Les Comédiennes adorées* (Paris: Dentu, 1873), p.248.

reward company members attending meetings with a silver token. Actresses with husbands in the company were excused attendance but still received their tokens. Following protests from actresses without husbands in the troupe, they too were excused. In the months that followed this decision, Mlle Guyot was the only actress ever to attend meetings, and that only periodically.[26]

How can we explain this gradual abandonment of equal rights on the part of actresses? I would suggest that it is linked to the changing status of actors as employees of the State. State intervention in theatre administration increased enormously between 1658 and 1683. During this time, a member of Molière's troupe, for example, would have gone from being a member of an independent provincial touring company to being a 'comédien du Roi', unable to take the least decision without the approval of the Premiers Gentilshommes de la Chambre. Were the women frozen out in this rigid régime of State control, or did they lose interest once all true autonomy had been taken from them, resigning themselves to the exploitation of their sexuality as their sole remaining area of influence? We will probably never know. In any event, a comparison of the Comédie-Française with the fairground theatres, which were considerably freer of State control, would seem to support this hypothesis of a correlation between State interference and the decline in women's influence. For, whereas women in the former institution were increasingly opting out of theatre administration as the century progressed, the fairgrounds were the domain of a number of extremely powerful women company directors; for example, Catherine Vondrebeck and Mme de Saint-Edmé.

Leaving aside the role played by women in theatre administration, is there anything left to say where actresses as performers are concerned? One aspect of particular interest is the relationship between their maternity and their professional lives. We have already seen De Pure's comment that too many actresses were too frequently pregnant for his taste, although not many would have equalled the comic actress Mlle Beauval's reputed twenty-eight children.[27]

Even so there must surely have been a considerable suspension of disbelief on the part of audiences when many actresses were playing young heroines, for once an actress had been given a role, she usually played it until death or retirement come what may. Moreover, it was unusual for an actress to be given an understudy. It was a rare occurrence indeed when on 16 August 1683 a replacement was arranged for Mlle Raisin in La Toison d'Or. And not before time — her son was baptized just five days later.[28] Nor was the outcome of performing while pregnant always fortunate. In 1721, Mlle Maillard died following a fairground performance in which, heavily pregnant, she was required to leap from a balcony onto the stage.[29] And attempting to end an unwanted pregnancy could end in tragedy for actresses as for so many others. Thus, Racine's former mistress Mlle Du Parc is widely believed to have died following an abortion attempt.[30]

Another serious matter generally ignored is the physical and sexual abuse to which young female performers, and even children,

26. S. Chevalley, 'Les Premières Assemblées des comédiens français', Mélanges de littérature et d'histoire offerts à Georges Couton (Lyon: Presses Universitaires, 1981), 443-51, p.445.

27. G. Mongrédien and J. Robert, Les Comédiens français du XVIIe siècle: dictionnaire biographique (Paris: CNRS, 1981), p.32.

28. Chevalley, 'Premières assemblées', p.447.

29. C and F Parfaict, Mémoire pour servir à l'histoire des spectacles de la foire, 2 vols (Paris: Briasson, 1743), Vol. I, pp.121-22.

30. C. Dulong, La Vie quotidienne des femmes au Grand Siècle (Paris: Hachette, 1984), p.183.

were occasionally subjected by fellow company members, particularly in the less well regulated fairground troupes which proliferated from the 1690s onwards. Examples of such behaviour, though, for the most part, fall outside the period currently in question.[31]

We have seen, therefore, that with very few exceptions, male commentators from the seventeenth to the early twentieth centuries have tended to concentrate their attention on certain aspects of women's participation in seventeenth-century theatre. Thus, they are almost invariably depicted as performers, exerting a powerful and frequently nefarious influence over all men with whom they came into contact, whether in a public or private sphere. Even so, little has been done until recently to present the reality of the lives of those women who worked in many different capacities in the professional theatre of the time. This leads me to suggest that it is only by both a careful re-examination of contemporary documents, and of the received wisdom of previous scholars, that we will be able to increase our knowledge of women's working conditions and come to a fuller appreciation of the diversity of their contribution to seventeenth-century French theatrical life.

31. See, for example, E. Campardon, *Les Spectacles de la Foire*, 2 vols (Geneva: Slatkine, 1970), Vol. II, pp.323-25.

Aphra Behn & the French Astrea: Madame de Villedieu

Elizabeth Woodrough

Elizabeth Woodrough is Lecturer in the Department of French at the University of Exeter

The late Frances Yates's classic study of the imperial theme of the Virgo-Astraea in England stops short of the full comparison with France, which, in other circumstances, she might have liked to have undertaken.[1] She notes in passing that early French representations of the starry goddess of justice, who abhorred the violence of men and whose return to earth heralded the Golden Age, are on occasion remarkably reminiscent of the symbolism of the Elizabethan age. This daughter of Zeus and Themis, a tiara of ears of corn upon her head like Ceres, was apparently the most constantly used symbol of Henri IV's reign. The frontispiece of Pierre Matthieu's *Histoire de France* (History of France) (1605), shows a regal figure looking much like Marie de Médicis seated on a throne, the crown of France supported on columns above her head, a wreathed sword in one hand, a cornucopia in the other, reminding us that the future Queen Regent had been invested with some at least of the majesty of the imperial English virgin. At her feet lie the symbols of the peaceful pursuit of the arts and sciences while, in the background, her subjects indulge in the sporting pleasures of both the tournament and the hunt.

As a new world of letters opened up to women, Astraea, symbol of eloquence, virginity and, paradoxically, also of fertility, provided a powerful source of poetic as well as political inspiration in both countries. Overlaid with Elizabethan associations, the name of the Greek goddess was also evoked by Dryden in the title of his celebratory poem in honour of Charles II's triumphant return from France in 1660, *Astraea Redux*. Further elevated in France by the publication of Ronsard's sonnet and madrigal cycle of Astrean conceits, her reappearance in Honoré D'Urfé's massive pastoral novel, *L'Astrée ou les divers effets de l'honneste amitié* (Astrea or the diverse effects of honest friendship) (1607-1624), celebrating the return of peace at the dawn of a new century, may be said to mark the beginning of a golden age in the early history of European feminism. A novel overflowing with sexual disguises, games and feints of one kind or another, *L'Astrée* became the standard reference for seventeenth-century novelists, poets and dramatists alike, including the occasional 'defenceless woman' who was prepared to play the 'masculine part' and write her own plays.

The prolific English Restoration playwright Aphra Behn's adoption of the anglicised version of this name as her *nom de plume*, can be directly related to the great respect in which d'Urfé's Fairie Queen of Forez, 'bright star of female virtue',[2] was held on both sides of the channel. Sometimes known only by the initials A.B., the writer's surname and Christian names offer innumerable

1. F.A. Yates, *Astraea: the Imperial Theme in the Sixteenth Century* (London and Boston: Routledge and Kegan Paul, 1975), p.82, n.2, and p.208 ff.
2. T. Killigrew, *Thomaso*, Part II, 5.10.125.

variations.[3] 'What are we to call her?', Vita Sackville-West mused in her biography of 1937: 'Aphra, Ayfara, Aphara, Aphora, Afra, Apharra, Afara, or, more fantastically, Aphaw or even Fyhare.'[4] One can see why Mrs Behn, Bhen or Beene, née Johnson or Amis, somewhere near Canterbury in Kent, should so readily have substituted that further variation upon a theme, the romantic Astrea, for the more prosaic Aphra, patron saint of prostitutes, a name associated with sin and penitence.

The first recorded instance of an allusion to this other 'fair shepherdess' comes in reports from the colony of Surinam in late 1663 and early 1664. The Deputy Governor, William Byam, writes ironically of a lady visitor who, having inspired the 'sympatheticall passion of the grand shepheard Celedon (sic)', after the hero of d'Urfé's novel — in this case one William Scot — was pursued by him when she returned to England early in 1664.[5] The pair actually used the code-names Astrea and Celadon, both by-words for disguise, again two years later when they were involved in a spying mission to Holland.

Having made an impression on Charles II with her account of her stay in the New World, which it has been suggested may itself have been a complete fiction, the recently widowed Mrs Behn was sent to Antwerp, on the recommendation of the playwright Thomas Killigrew, to persuade Scot to turn double agent and inform on both the Dutch and the English insurrectionaries in Holland. Whatever the success of her mission, it seems that the English authorities did not take her reports very seriously. It was thus that she 'came to learn early on in life that the roles of a woman writer and political commentator were incompatible in the public mind.'[6] As so frequently in such cases of service to King and country, the couple were disappointed by the 'slendernesse of theire rewards' and Mrs Behn makes a further reference in her correspondence to having to pawn her rings to pay her uncharacteristically mercenary Celadon. On her return the shepherdess-spy was temporarily imprisoned for debts incurred in the King's service, making her entrance into theatrical work where she had influential contacts, a financial imperative.

Astrea became Mrs Behn's preferred name as a professional writer. The register in Westminster Abbey, where she is buried, reads simply 'Mrs Astrea Behn'. It was also as Astrea that she was reincarnated early the following century by Delarivier Manley in her major scandal novel, *The New Atalantis* (1709).[7] During her lifetime Mrs Behn signed much of her correspondence in this way, as well as the dedicatory preface to her translation of La Rochefoucauld's *Maximes* (1685). This text, together with her translations of a number of French novels and *nouvelles*, like Paul Tallemant's *Voyage de l'Isle d'amour* (Voyage to the Island of Love) (1684) and Fontenelle's treatise of popular astronomy, *Entretiens sur la pluralité des mondes* (Conversations on the plurality of worlds) (1689), testifies to the depth of her interest in contemporary French literature and to her knowledge of the French language, possibly learned from Huguenot refugees in Kent.[8]

3. Janet Todd suggests that we are possibly dealing with two women, baptised Ann or Anne, both used at different moments as pseudonyms by Aphra/ Astrea. See *Works of Aphra Behn*, ed. by J. Todd (London: Pickering and Chatto, 1992), Vol I, xxx, n.2.

4. V. Sackville West, *Aphra Behn: The Incomparable Astrea* (London: Howe, 1937), p.11.

5. See Todd, *The Works of Aphra Behn*, Vol.I, ix.

6. R. Ballaster, 'Pretences of State: Aphra Behn and the Female Plot', in *Rereading Aphra Behn: History, Theory and Criticism*, ed. H. Hunter (University Press of Virginia, 1993), pp. 187-211, p. 190.

7. See R. Ballaster, *Seductive Forms: Women's Amatory Fiction from 1684 to 1740* (Oxford: Clarendon Press, 1992), p.114.

8. J. Jones, 'New Light on Aphra Behn', *Notes and Queries*, Vol.37 (September 1990), 235-6, 235.

Her literary pseudonym has not been much in favour with those rereading her work of late, but the French connection which it suggests may yet yield a more rounded picture of this mysterious figure who, in the words of her most recent editor, Janet Todd, 'refuses to reveal a single plausible life.'[9]

For too long valued primarily on account of her status as the first woman openly to acknowledge her works and to earn her living by her pen, Mrs Behn was regarded simply as: 'a colossal and enduring embarrassment to the generations of women who followed her into the literary market-place — an ancestress to be lived down rather than lived up to, who seemed in Virginia Woolf's metaphor, to obstruct the very passageway to the profession of letters she had herself opened.'[10] Her plays, poetry and fiction are now gradually gaining wider recognition, and interest can only increase as the various volumes of Janet Todd's new edition of her complete works appear. By no means the first English woman dramatist, Astrea/Aphra was the author of between seventeen and nineteen plays, confirming by her prodigious output her belief that, with the exception of Dryden, there were, 'none that write at such a formidable rate, but that a woman may well hope to reach their greatest heights'.

It has been argued that it was 'To enable herself to write, [that] Behn created a poetic identity for herself as Astrea, muse of a lost golden age who could combine "Female Sweetness and a Manly Grace" [... and that] to avoid becoming the disdainful lady or the disdained whore of male polarization, [she] identified with the male role while modifying its view of women.'[11] There was certainly much in the provocative sexual ambiguity of d'Urfé's feminist *bergerie* (sheepfold) to fascinate and inspire the exotic, mythologising, 'double-dressing' poet/playwright, so fond of exploiting and confounding traditional gender roles in her life and work. Her own vision of a prelapsarian golden age, where women had enjoyed the same status as men, echoes to the strains of d'Urfé's Forezian paradise.

In the opening pages of *L'Astrée*, first translated extensively into English in 1657-8, the heroine issues an imperious command with all the authority of the Queen of England, forbidding her lover, Céladon, from appearing again before her in the Arcadian forests of Forez until she orders him so to do:

'VA-T-EN, ET GARDE-TOI BIEN DE JAMAIS TE FAIRE VOIR A MOI QUE JE NE TE LE COMMANDE'.

(Be gone with you, and do not dare to appear before me again until I order you so to do.)[12]

Ever the willing subject, Céladon swiftly circumvents the problem by changing gender and disguising himself as the druidess, Alexis. Through this humorous reinterpretation of the letter of Astrean law, the hero comes to enjoy the most tantalising proximity to his mistress, sharing her bed, helping her dress and undress and kissing her breast with more than sisterly affection whenever the occasion presents

9. Todd, *The Works of Aphra Behn*, I, ix. On the French connection, see also E. Brinks, 'Meeting over the map: Madeleine de Scudery's *Carte du Pays de Tendre* and Aphra Behn's *Voyaqe de l'Isle d'amour* (1684), *Studies in English Literary Culture 1660-1700*, No.17, pp.39-52.

10. C. Gallagher, 'Who was that masked woman? The prostitute and the playwright in the comedies of Aphra Behn', *Rereading Aphra Behn*, pp.65-85, p.65.

11. See R. Ballaster, *Seductive Forms*, pp.72-3.

12. H. d'Urfé, *L'Astree*, ed. M. Gaume (Saint-Etienne, Le Hénaff, 1980), p.30.

itself.   In the later volumes, d'Urfé plays with a mildly erotic feminisation of the open-ended narrative he would never live to complete himself, by introducing an ambivalent use of feminine forms to designate both hero and heroine, as is illustrated in the following extract describing the couple's new bedtime ritual:

> *Quant à Alexis, s'étant un peu relevée sur le lit, elle aidait à Astrée, luy ôtant tantôt un noeud, et tantôt une épingle, et si quelquefois sa main passait près de la bouche d'Astrée, elle la lui baisait, et Alexis, feignant de ne vouloir qu'elle lui fît cette faveur, rebaisait incontinent le lieu où sa bouche avait touché si ravie de contentment que Léonide prenait un plaisir extrême de la voir en cet excès de bonheur.*

> (As for Alexis, who had sat up a little in bed, she was helping Astrée, undoing a knot here and a pin there, and if occasionally her hand brushed against Astrée's mouth, she would kiss it, and Alexis, pretending not to desire any such favour, straightway kissed the place where her lips had been, so deliriously happy that Leonide took an extreme delight in seeing her in such ecstacy.)[13]

In the novel Céladon/Alexis disguises him/herself as Astrée, and Astrée disguises herself as Alexis in a series of sexual metamorphoses no more and no less strange than the sequence of changes from male to female and back again in *The Young King*, which Behn said was the first play she ever wrote. Similarly, in the 1677 performance of *The Constant Nymph* she had her actress friend Elizabeth Barry play the pastoral hero in the guise of a shepherdess, the better to woo an Astrea determined never to marry. This and other provocative poetic allusions in Behn's work fit well with the teasingly erotic mood of parts of d'Urfé's novel.

One of the first French texts to give added value to the female sex as desiring narrative subjects and as narrators, *L'Astrée* also inspired generations of French women to exploit their own potential as writers. Read and reread as a manual of *politesse* (urbanity) and sexual relations in the burgeoning salons hosted by the Marquise de Rambouillet and the Grande Mademoiselle, who sought to act out just such a pastoral idyll in the grounds of their castles at Rambouillet near Paris and Saint-Fargeau in the Yonne, this cult novel was one of the factors encouraging women of lesser rank, like Madeleine de Scudéry, to write their own great fictional fantasies about the female-dominated *salon* societies in the 1650s, before the resurgence of court society under Louis XIV made it impossible for women to ignore the fact, even in fiction, that men were only very rarely prepared to treat the opposite sex with the reverence due to goddesses. If *L'Astrée* remained a constant source of inspiration in the second half of the century, its idealism had become untenable, as the work of the rare women dramatists of the period attests.[14]

The vices and virtues of French seventeenth-century women's fictions inside and outside the Urféen tradition from *Cyrus* to *La Princesse de Clèves* have been exhaustively documented in the last decade. Their pioneering achievements as dramatists prepared to compete openly with male writers during Louis XIV's reign are

13. Ibid., p.210.
14. See P. Gethner, 'Melpomene meets women playwrights in the Age of Louis XIV', *Neophilogus* (1988), 72, pp.17-33.

only now being recognised, thanks largely to the efforts of American scholars, less impressed by the canonical interpretation of Classicism with a capital C. It is true that the few women who wrote plays in seventeenth-century France were all reluctant dramatists, who remain better known for their novels, short tales or poetry. Popular women novelists were content for the most part to let male dramatists turn their fiction into plays. The latest bibliography of early French women dramatists reveals that of the twenty-six French female dramatists listed between 1650 and 1750, sixteen wrote no more than one or two plays, like most of Mrs Behn's English contemporaries, with the exception of Margaret Cavendish, Duchess of Newcastle.[15] No French woman wrote more than three plays which were actually performed. Many of their plays were what were known in England as 'closet dramas' and never intended for public performance. Of the thirty-three plays written by French women before 1700, eleven were probably never performed, and several were never published and have since been lost. It is not, therefore, surprising that comparisons with women dramatists of other nationalities have so far gone largely unremarked.

Yet there is a lone star in the firmament of early French women's theatre who may be measured against the yardstick of England's Incomparable Astrea, though she is now, like all the other French women writers of the time, better known for her letters and fiction. Marie-Catherine Desjardins was an exact contemporary of Aphra Behn, probably born in the same year, 1640, in the town of Alençon in Normandy. Always anxious to sign her works as Mme de Villedieu, though she was never actually married to her soldier-lover, Antoine Boësset de Villedieu,[16] Mlle Desjardins usurped many of Aphra Behn's theatrical 'firsts'. During the highly competitive first decade of Louis XIV's personal reign, she enjoyed a brief — but spectacular — career in the Parisian theatre. It was all over by the time she was twenty-five, a full five years before Mrs Behn launched her long dramatic career with two tragi-comedies with French-inspired titles, The Forc'd Marriage and The Amorous Prince. Mme de Villedieu was in fact the first French woman

15. See *Les Femmes dramaturges en France (1650-1750). Pièces choisies*, ed. P. Gethner (Paris, Seattle, Tübingen: PFSCL Biblio 17, 1993), pp.18-21. This is now available in translation: *The Lunatic Lover: Seventeenth- and Eighteenth-Century French Plays by Women Writers*, ed. P. Gethner (Heinemann, 1994).

16. Villedieu in fact forced her to sign a declaration to the effect that no marriage had ever been contracted. See ibid., p.60.

Mme de Villedieu   (By kind permission of Mercure de France)

to have her plays professionally performed in the capital, the first to have her work reviewed in a Gazette, and also the first to receive a command performance in the gardens at Versailles, accompanied by all the pomp and circumstance, and special effects, of the Molière-centred *divertissements* (entertainments) that had just begun to bring the '*fertiles déserts*' of the King's new castle to life in the week-long Drama Festival of the *Plaisirs de l'Ile enchantée* (Pleasures of the Enchanted Isle) the previous year.

Of slightly higher social status than the merchant's (or possibly slave trader's) widow, Mrs Behn, whose husband was also a very shadowy figure, Mrs de Villedieu is no less of an enigma. Every fact of her life has been contested. Nevertheless, it is fair to say that she too was dogged by financial problems, though she never found herself in quite such desperate straits as her English counterpart. After the legal separation of her parents when she was 20, Mlle Desjardins turned to writing to help support her mother and sister, becoming as prolific in fiction as her English counterpart was in the theatre. Obliged to depend on her own resources for most of her life, her career offers many interesting parallels with that of Aphra Behn. Equally well schooled in passionate suffering, she also began as a poet, wrote a fascinating series of love letters which would be made public, and eventually turned from the theatre back to fiction as a more lucrative genre, dabbling with fables along the way.[17] As both wrote, in the words of Alpha Behn, 'to earn their bread', and neither was ashamed to admit it, they naturally opened themselves up to the old 'writer-as-newfangled-whore' view of the woman writer. Capitalising on such prejudices, Mrs Behn, who was constantly accused of immorality on and off the stage, knew how to exploit this persona, amongst others, to her own advantage by framing her plays 'within the larger comedy of erotic exchange between a woman writer and male audience'[18].

Mme de Villedieu was no less vulnerable to personal attack, and no less able to use her sexual misadventures to her own advantage. In his early pen portrait of her, the mischevious social chronicler, Tallemant des Réaux tells us that she read her suggestive first sonnet on the theme of *jouissance* (pleasure) out loud in the salons with immodest passion. Tallemant cannot deny her talent, but makes as public as he can the fact that at the beginning of their affair, '*elle coucha avec Villedieu trois mois durant assez publiquement*' (She slept with Villedieu quite publicly for three months). Including as many details as he can gather from hearsay, Tallemant gives as proof of this that they were seen in bed together exchanging shirts early one morning.[19] Like Behn's bisexual lover — the Gray's Inn lawyer, John Hoyle — Villedieu was forever trying to escape his mistress's attention, eventually marrying another, and making her the victim of what Mrs Behn might have called a fair jilt.[20]

Little daunted, Desjardin/Villedieu, as she occasionally signed her name, continued to romanticise her affair with her lover on the stage and in fiction. She comes closest to recognising the truth of the situation in *La Vie d'Henriette-Sylvie de Molière* (*The Life of Henriette-Sylvie de Molière*) (1671), where she appropriated the male

17. Aphra Behn produced an edition of *Aesop's Fables* in English, French and Latin; Mme de Villedieu presented a collection of fables to Louis XIV, though they have also been attributed to La Fontaine.

18. Gallagher, 'Who was that masked woman?', *Rereading Aphra Behn*, p.66.

19. G. Tallemant des Réaux, *Historiettes*, ed. A. Adam (Pléiade, 1960), II, pp.900-909.

20. M. Cuénin, *Roman et Société sous Louis XIV: Madame de Villedieu (Marie-Catherine Des jardins (1640-1683)*, (University of Lille: Champion, 1979), 2 vols, I, pp.38-39.

aristocratic genre of memoirs to rewrite her scandalous little tale one more time under a transparent pseudonym reminiscent of her days in the theatre. In scenes of Urféen complexity, the picaresque heroine of this tale and the women she meets on her travels are forced to act and dress as men in order to make their way in and around the world, giving rise to endless cases of mistaken sexual identity. One of the earliest examples of pseudo-memoirs, the text seems at times to come very close to autobiography. Mlle de Molière's secret second marriage to the Comte d'Englessac is not recognised in society; she is persecuted by his family when she becomes pregnant, and her child dies; her husband dies too, but not without a public declaration of undying love for a Greek woman encountered on his travels, causing Mlle Molière further embarrassment.

By exposing both these women writers to this kind of public ridicule in real life, the irregular relationships with Villedieu and Hoyle seem to have been essential preparation for their involvement in the theatre, pushing them beyond the forms of writing which favoured the anonymity and privacy considered more suitable to the female sex, as well as encouraging them to break new barriers in their writing of fiction, letters, and poetry. With her innovations in fiction, Mme de Villedieu was again always a few years ahead of her English counterpart. Her capacity to deceive readers by the invention of true lies in works that she called *nouvelles historiques* (historical novellas), exploiting devices that were to become familiar in Aphra Behn's variations on the 'little history' is notorious.[21] Yet, if in Aphra Behn's criticism, the name of Mme de Villedieu is sometimes cited in passing as one of a number of French women novelist precursors, no mention is made of the fact that she alone among them also wrote plays.

Although she did not write as many plays and they differ in almost every respect from the sexual farces for which Aphra Behn is famed, Mme de Villedieu's impact on French audiences should not be underestimated. Her three dramatic poems were in fact performed in the most illustrious of Parisian theatres. The first, *Manlius Torquatus* (1662), a tragi-comedy, was staged at the Hôtel de Bourgogne by the King's troupe. It was a moderate success, controversial enough in its happy ending, contradicting the facts of the Roman legend (where the hero was put to death by his father's hand) to place the author momentarily at the centre of a critical debate about *vraisemblance* (credibility) of the kind essential to the launch of a dramatist's career at the time. The principal protagonists were two giants of the French theatrical scene, Pierre Corneille (Mme de Villedieu's principal source) and the abbot d'Aubignac, the most important dramatic theorist of the seventeenth century, who had become Villedieu's theatrical mentor and to whom Mrs Behn makes a brief reference in the preface to *The Lucky Chance* (1686). The acidic d'Aubignac regarded *Manlius* practically as his own, and Mme de Villedieu became a pawn in his all out attack on the author of *Sertorius* and *Sophonisbe*. In his remarks on yet another new play by the master, the *abbé* went so far as to accuse the great Corneille of authorial envy:

21. See R. Ballaster, *Seductive Forms*, p.53.

Vous avez une étrange aversion contre Mlle Desjardins; il vous fâche qu'une fille vous dame le pion et vous lui voulez dérober son Manlius par l'effet d'une jalousie sans exemple.

(You have taken a strange dislike to Mlle Desjardins: you are annoyed that a mere girl should outplay you in this way and you want to steal her Manlius away from her because you are so extraordinarily jealous.)

Nitétis (1663), Mme de Villedieu's second play, a Scudérian hymn to female heroism, was a resounding flop, though it was staged in the same august surroundings and several favourable accounts appeared in print, including a complimentary notice in Jean Loret's gazette, *La Muse Historique.*

Le Favori (*The Favourite*) (1665), Mme de Villedieu's final court spectacular, which ran to twenty-six performances in all at the Palais Royal from the 24 April 1665 to the 17 August 1666, was another tragicomedy, which originally went by the double reverse title, *Le Favori, ou la Coquette.* Its Parisian success is in part to be explained by the fact that after seventeen separate performances, new and old Molière farces were added to the programme, according to Molière's own practice, whenever he wanted to extend the life of a play. Its performance at court half-way through this run would also have redoubled the interest of Parisian audiences. The plot had clearly been devised with an eye to a court audience. The theme of favouritism and jealousy at the court of the King of Barcelona set in an indefinable present may be seen as an allegory of the misfortunes of Nicolas Fouquet, Louis XIV's minister of Finance, whose trial was the social and political sensation of 1664. The sentence he received, exile changed to life imprisonment at the King's request, was pronounced between the composition and the performance of Mme de Villedieu's play, which had been delayed by a year while the author went off to the South of France, on money borrowed from Molière, to bid her lover farewell before he sailed with the French fleet. The exile of Ministers was thus a subject of some topicality. Mme de Villedieu was of course in no position to offend the King, even had she hoped to defend Fouquet.[22]

Le Favori is in fact one of those intriguing cases in French classical theatre of a play which deals with issues that might be thought too close to political actuality for comfort, but nonetheless clearly met with royal approval. Even had the play been intended as a direct allusion to Fouquet, it might not have made much difference. Fouquet, who had begun the series of festival plays by commanding Molière to write *Les Fâcheux* (*The Bores*) for the King's pleasure in 1661, and been designated as principal court bore by Louis XIV as soon as the party was over, was in any case always a good subject for such theatrical events.

The command performance of *Le Favori* at Versailles on the evening of 13 June 1665, under the direction of the Duc de Saint-Aignan, was undertaken by Molière's troupe, then at the height of their fame and theatrical controversy following the first version of *Tartuffe* and *Dom Juan*, and only recently appointed the *Troupe du*

22. See *Les Femmes dramaturges,* p.64.

roi (The King's troupe). As with his own command performances, Molière *'entremêla [la pièce] d'intermèdes et d'entrées de ballet, avec concert de voix et instruments'* (introduced interludes and ballet scenes, with a concert of voices and instruments). As had become standard practice on such occasions, Lully composed the music and accompanying vocals, and an impressive Vigarini garden stage-set was constructed to complement the outdoor setting, which Mme de Villedieu described as having

> *trois théâtres de verdure sous les portiques, séparés par des lignes de hauts cyprès en pyramides: les décors de la scène centrale s'ouvraient sur un jardin en espalier; vases de porcelaine, girandoles de cristal, cascades sautant des rochers, allées illuminées [...].*

> (three garden stages set up under the porticos, separated by lines of high pyramid-shaped cypress trees: the centre stage-sets opened onto a garden with espaliers; porcelain vases, crystal water jets, waterfalls, illuminated walks [...]).[23]

For this court version of *Le Favori,* Molière wrote a special prologue. Now lost, this kind of illusionist impromptu beginning had been used to much effect to disorientate the royal spectators the previous year in the 'royal rehearsal' play, *L'Impromptu de Versailles.* La Grange's record of the event reads:

> *Mr de Molière fit un prologue en marquis ridicule qui voulait être sur le théâtre malgré les gardes, et eut une conversation risible avec une actrice qui fit la marquise ridicule, placée au milieu de l'assemblée.*[24]

> (Molière performed the prologue, disguised as a ridiculous marquess whom the guards could not keep off the stage, and held a ridiculous conversation with an actress who was similarly attired who had been planted in the middle of the audience).

Molière's framing of Mme de Villedieu's play was thus designed to do humorous homage to the playwright and her sex. It also offered the noble spectators the closer involvement in the theatrical experience that was clearly appreciated at court. The missing prologue to *Le Favori* sounds worthy of comparison with Aphra Behn's prologue to her first play, *The Forc'd Marriage,* with its Molière-inspired title, where a male actor pretends to have escaped temporarily from the control of the intriguing woman playwright, who joins the other women in the audience and warns the gallants beside them of the dangerous new weapon which women now hold in their amorous arsenal: the art of playwrighting.

Mme de Villedieu's parting shot at Versailles in the summer of 1665, which was completed by a collation and prefaced by a ball or ballet on the garden stage and brought to a close by a firework display, was favourably recorded in the Gazettes of the day in a way that again shows how similar the condition of the early woman playwright may be on two sides of the channel. It is recorded how:

23. M. Cuénin, *Roman et Societé*, I, pp.221, n.75
24. *Les Femmes dramaturges*, p.68.

> *'Après le bal, la comédie/ Divertit bien la compagnie/ Ouvrage parfait et chéri/ Intitulé* Le Favory */ Composé de la main savante / De cette personne charmante / Qui dans un beau corps féminin / Enferme un esprit masculin.'*

(After the ball came the play which amused the company very well, a perfect dear work, called *The Favourite* / composed by the clever hand of that charming person who in a beautiful female body encloses a masculine mind.)[25]

The by-now famous concluding paragraph to *The Lucky Chance*, where Mrs Behn laid down a heart-felt challenge to all who would deny her freedom of expression, has echoes of this view of the woman writer as a kind of hermaphrodite:

'All I ask is the privilege for my masculine part the poet in me (if any such you will allow me), to tread in those successful paths my predecessors have so long thrived in, to take those measures that both the ancient and modern writers have set me, and by which they have pleased the world so well. If I must not, because of my sex, have this freedom, but that you will usurp all to yourselves; I lay down my quill and you shall hear no more of me.'

After this play, Mrs Behn turned increasingly to fiction, and as the London theatres found themselves in increasing financial difficulties. The King's theatre company closed; the Duke's Company, who had performed many of her comedies, staged fewer new plays. Internal disputes were rife, and following the 'discovery' of the Popish plot there was a general decline in theatre-going.[26]

Mme de Villedieu's decision to write no more plays at a time when the French theatre was at its most dynamic and she had just managed to bring her work to the attention of the King is rather more puzzling. Her relationship with the court seems to have been fairly well established. She was, in fact, already a kind of self-appointed court correspondent. Within four days of the court production of *Le Favori*, she had again (with the duc de Saint-Aignan's encouragement) produced a *Description d'une des fêtes que le Roi donna à Versailles* (Description of one of the festivals which the King gave in Versailles); in the event, her own.

As befits their status as professional writers, both Villedieu and Behn were well versed in the art of the prefatory dedication. The networks of influential patrons which they established at court are very similar. Where one sought the support of — among others — the Duke of York (Charles II's illegitimate son), Henry Fitzroy and the Earl of Rochester, the other addressed her plays to the King's niece, the Grande Mademoiselle, Saint-Aignan and M. de Lionne. Lionne died before he could offer his full assistance to Mme de Villedieu, but he nevertheless recommended this lady dramatist for the singular honour of a royal pension, which was eventually paid at a much reduced rate many years later. Astrea's relations with the great are rather less certain, although she seems to have had some familiarity with the Earl of Rochester and his merry gang of courtly wits, and was one of the staunchest apologists for Stuart Kings. She had also managed to offend Charles II by her allusion to Monmouth, as we have seen. If her *Pindarick on the Coronation* of James II never earned her the fine house and garden she might have been expecting, she seems at least to have been paid by the court for her services in

25. Cuénin, *Roman et société*, pp.124–5, n.76.
26. See R. Ballaster, '"Pretences of State": Aphra Behn and the Female Plot', in *Rereading Aphra Behn*, pp.187–211, p.187.

writing what she herself called 'Tory farce and Dogerell', but not enough to keep her when the theatre no longer brought her public patronage.[27]

It does not seem excessive then to see in Mme de Villedieu a kind of French Astrea, who was by some standards even more successful as a dramatist than her English counterpart. Such *noms de guerre* (pseudonyms) were all the rage in seventeenth-century France, although Astrea might not have been the obvious choice for Marie-Catherine Desjardins, who seems to have preferred to think of herself as an Iris. The portrait of her pock-marked face reproduced here, so much less attractive than the well-known Mary Beale portrait of Aphra, confirms a reputation for ugliness that would have made it more difficult for her to pretend to such fair names in anything but fiction. She was in any case an Astrea, or rather an Iris, so entirely obsessed by her '*infidelle Clidamis*' (unfaithful Clidamis), the pseudonym she uses for her romantic portrait of Villedieu in the novel *Anaxandre* (1667), that she wished only to use her public notoriety as a writer to establish herself if not as the latter's wife, then at least as his widow, by changing her surname to his.

All the texts of the plays in fact bear the name of Mlle Desjardins. Tallemant tells us that she had asked to be known by the name Villedieu on the *affiches* (playbills) announcing the performances of *Le Favori*, when she returned from her travels in Southern France. But Molière objected, agreeing to call her by the name '*partout hormis sur le théâtre et dans ses affiches*' (Everywhere except on the stage and on the playbills).'[28] She only finally managed to impose the name on her publishers and public, apparently with the family's consent, after Villedieu's death on the battlefield in 1667 at the siege of Lille, by which time her rake lover had a different wife and Mlle Desjardins had herself given up the theatre for novels and *nouvelles*. When publishing her two-volume novella *Carmante* later that year, Claude Barbin felt it necessary to remind readers that the Mme de Villedieu on the cover was also the '*Auteur de Manlius*' (Author of Manlius) under a different name.

Any detailed analysis of the three Desjardins/de Villedieu plays can only underline how little her theatre has in common with the dramatic works of the English Astrea. Another of life's unfortunate experts in the disorders of love, Mme de Villedieu makes '*la folle passion*' (mad passion) and '*la bouillante ardeur*' (hot love) no less the subject of her drama than of her fiction, but not always recognisably so for those who do not take into account the full range of her novels and *nouvelles*. *Alcidamie*, her first novel, was actually conceived as the kind of interminable lovers' idyll so popular in the multi-volumed novels of the first half of the century from *L'Astrée* to *Clélie*, but ever sensitive to changing fashions, she abandoned it after two volumes in favour of the short and increasingly bitter tales of disappointed love, deceit and betrayal which became the hallmark of her work. As her theatre belongs to the early part of her career and mirrors the idealism of her fiction during this period, it cannot easily be compared with Mrs Behn's work of the 1670s and 1680s, full of 'rakes, bosoms, trysts, masks, and swords'.[29]

27. See *Behn: Five Plays*, ed. M. Duffy (London: Methuen, 1990), xi
28. 'Tallemant des Réaux', *Historiettes*, II, p.907.
29. A. Behn, *The Rover (The Banished Cavaliers)*, (London: Methuen, 1987), p.17.

The heroes and heroines of Mme de Villedieu's plays, inspired by Corneille, tempered by a reading of classical history which owes much to the *préciosité* (preciosity) of Mlle de Scudéry, are perhaps closer to the exemplary morality of the work of English woman dramatists of the turn of the century, such as Catherine Trotter, Delariviere Manley, and Mary Pix, than to the bawdy dialogue of Behn's comedies and farces, with her lecherous men and dissembling women. The Cornelian *Manlius* is no *Rover* Parts One or Two, and there is a world of difference between the Molièresque comedy *The Favorite* and Mrs Behn's comedy of intrigue *The Feigned Courtesans,* though both are based on Spanish models. The virile young hero of the first play is merely a romanticised Villedieu, conquering all in dedication to his love for Omphale, with no trace in him of the Willmore/Mountebank deceiver who vainly tries to control and constrain the women he meets, which might have been nearer the mark. In their various disguises as boys and courtesans, the freedom-seeking Marcella, Cornelia and Laura Lucretia could give lessons in outspoken feminism to the bookish but adoring Lindamire, the virtuous heroine of *Le Favori*, whose highest ambition is to abandon everything for the love of one man.

Mrs Behn's teasing claim in the preface to *Sir Patient Fancy* that neither on the stage, nor on the page, would her play give 'the most innocent Virgins [...] cause to blush' might fairly be applied to the whole of to Mme de Villedieu's theatre, though we know that her personal conduct offended the good women of Bruxelles, among others, during her stay there in 1667 when she visited the scientist Huyghens. In the decade before her death in 1680, the French dramatist and novelist was, as we have seen, herself writing with a new sexual realism, though she was no longer writing plays. *Les Annales galantes* and other of her *nouvelles* were, however, like Behn's most famous novel, *Oronooko,* successfully made into stage plays by others towards the end of the century.

It could be argued that when it comes to tragedy the similarities between the two women's plays are more striking. The theme of male tyranny is common to both *Nitetis* and Behn's only tragedy *Abelezar* (1685), but 'Love is very differently Arm'd' in Mme de Villedieu's play. Whereas Behn's Spanish Queen, Isabelle, is humiliated by the disdainful and calculating Moor, who seduces and rebuffs her, Nitétis emerges as the true hero(ine) of the play. A combination of Corneille's Pauline and Mlle de Scudéry's Clélie, she never allows her pure and innocent love for an entirely virtuous prince to interfere with her allegiance to honour and duty, though she is sorely tried by her evil husband, Cambyses. Nitétis openly admits her love for another, but insists like Corneille's Chimène: '*j'aime encore plus ma gloire*' (I love glory still more).

As *Le Favori* illustrates, even such common comic inspiration as might be found in Molière and the *commedia dell'arte* tradition does not bring the two Astreas much closer together. Whereas Aphra Behn is known for her bold farces like *The Emperor of the Moon* (1687), one of her greatest successes, and her bawdy interpretations of plays like *Le Malade Imaginaire*, Mme de Villedieu was not a comic author and clearly did not wish to be classed as such. Her choice of the outdated classification *tragicomédie* (tragicomedy) for *Le Favori* reassures the audience that there will be a happy ending, while dissociating the play from the greater prejudice against the lowly dramatic genre of farce. Her observation of the fickleness of courtiers, is not without its humorous moments, but is possibly at its most comic when the King of Barcelona declares his passion for his favourite in terms which, if taken literally, would have horrified the deeply heterosexual Louis XIV.

Nevertheless, it was farce that had first attracted Mme de Villedieu to the theatre and farce which first brought her to the attention of Molière and it is ultimately her relationship to his work, which was clearly also one of Mrs Behn's many influences, which reveals Mme de Villedieu's potential as a dramatist. She enjoys the distinction of having worked more closely with Molière than any other dramatist. Her earliest 'theatrical work', entitled '*Le récit en vers et en prose de la farce des Précieuses*' (a prose and verse account of the farce of the Précieuses) was in fact a witty overnight review of Molière's first Parisian play, where she dramatises the experience of the reviewer by pretending that she has not seen the play herself, but must rely on a friend's second-hand account. The closer her professional relationship with Molière became, the more determined she seems to have been to distance her own plays from any suggestion of comic vulgarity. Working with Molière and his production team at Versailles ensured Mme de Villedieu a higher profile as a dramatist than she could possibly have managed on her own. Just as comparisons between plays such as *The Rover* and Thomas Killigrew's *Thomaso* enrich our understanding of Behn's text,[30] so an analysis of the play which Molière helped Mlle Desjardins produce for the royal gaze allows us to evaluate her talent as a dramatist against the work of one of the greatest theatrical geniuses of her day. They also allow us to imagine a more complete life for her as a working dramatist than would be possible from the texts of her plays alone, which are remarkably free of the concerns of the practising dramatist revealed in Behn's prefaces.

Le Favori may in fact be seen as a kind of half-way house between *Les Fâcheux*, Molière's first command performance and *Le Misanthrope ou l'atrabilaire* (*The Misanthropist*), one of his finest and most refined comedies, itself a reworking of *Dom Garcie de Navarre*. Some have seen in Mme de Villedieu's play the inspiration for *Le Misanthrope* which was performed a year later, though there is some evidence that the first act, which is perhaps the closest in structure to *Le Favori*, had been already written by July 1664 when Molière's troupe first accepted Mme de Villedieu's play for performance. Although Mme de Villedieu's play is dismissed as inferior by Molière critics, the two plays are worthy of comparison as social satires since they are amongst the first to deal directly with the complexities of social relations among courtiers competing for attention. Many of the characters and several of the scenes are reminiscent of each other, although Molière's play views the court indirectly through the salon. Moncade is just as depressed about the insincerity of social relations

30. See H. Hunter, 'Revisioning the female body: Aphra Behn's *The Rover*, Parts I and II', in *Rereading Aphra Behn*, pp. 102–120

as the black-biled Misanthrop, Alceste. Philinte, Célimène, Oronte and Emilie all find their equivalents in Mme de Villedieu's play. The plays differ to the extent that though he may be ready enough to embrace it, Moncade's trial exile is not, as we have seen, self-imposed like Alceste's. In a scene as reminiscent of the closing scenes of *Le Cid* as the end of *Le Misanthrope*, Moncade's mistress declares herself, like Emilie, willing to accompany him into the desert of exile, while D. Elvire, a kind of Célimène *avant la lettre* quickly transfers her allegiance:

> *Je sais ce qu'est la gloire et le parfait amour: Mais je crains la disgrâce, et j'aime fort la cour.*

> (I know what glory and perfect love are. But I fear disgrace and I like the court too well.)[31]

When the King reveals in a *coup de théâtre* that Moncade's disgrace was but a little play-acting on his part to test the loyalty of his friend, Lindamire prepared to risk disgrace for love, naturally emerges — like Nitetitis — as the only hero(ine) in the play..

Whatever the order in which *Le Favori* and *Le Misanthrope* were written, it remains just as fascinating to imagine Molière (whose collaboration with a new playwright in whatever capacity could only add to their reputation) using his recent experience of the tricks of the command performance to help Mme de Villedieu with her first court play, as to prove that *Le Misanthrope*, like so many other male masterpieces, was a direct borrowing from a woman's lesser *oeuvre*. In any case, since originality was never the soul of comedy, it is interesting to note that the comic playwright was busy reading and reinterpreting Tirso de Molina's *El Burlador* (The Trickster) for *Dom Juan*, at the same time that his new female colleague was working on Molina's *El Amor y Amistad* (Love and Friendship) for her own *pièce de résistance*.

The question remains why at the height of her career, when she had received the highest honours a dramatist might be accorded, and was classed by some with MM. Corneille le Jeune, Desmarets, Molière, Quinault, and Racine, did Mme de Villedieu, so prolific in other genres, suddenly abandon the theatre altogether in favour of fiction just as Mrs Behn was about to embark on her theatrical *oeuvre*? Did she sense herself unequal to the competition with the arrival on the scene of Racine to complete the great trilogy of male dramatists of the classical age? Did Molière, anxious to get on with his own career at court and battling with the overweening ambitions of his musical collaborator, Lully, and his own increasing ill-health, withdraw his active support? Was Mme de Villedieu, embarrassed as we know by d'Aubignac's insistence on championing her cause when he was himself long past his prime, simply oppressed by the fact that a woman could not hope to work independently in the male dominated world of the theatre? Was she insufficiently committed to a dramatic career, as implied by her flight from Paris when *Le Favori* was ready for performance? Did she simply recognise the new fiction where women writers were in the ascendant as a more

31. M.-C. Desjardins, *Le Favori*, in *Les Femmes dramaturges*, p.107.

lucrative market and one where she could at last write about the realities of love for women at the French court?

In a letter dated 12 June, 1667, Mme de Villedieu refers to a tragedy entitled *Agis* which she was then writing and presumably never finished.[32] 1667 might be termed her *annus mirabilis* or rather *annus horribilis*: that was the summer that her lover was killed in battle, but not before he had sealed their separation by selling her love letters to Barbin for publication. That she was greatly distressed at this further public demonstration of Villedieu's disloyalty is confirmed by the fact that she insisted that these *Lettres et billets galants*,which reveal a deeply sensitive soul, should be published anonymously.

In the absence of any kind of theoretical reflection on the part of Mme de Villedieu or other French women dramatists on the status of women, or the craft of writing for the theatre, such personal motives seem to offer as valid an explanation as any other. Perry Gethner has remarked on the difference between the English and French in this respect:

> *Même entre 1650 et 1750, où nous trouvons un nombre considérable de femmes auteurs qui réussirent à faire jouer leurs pièces par des acteurs professionnels et à les publier de leur vivant, il est difficile de discerner beaucoup d'interaction. Par exemple, combien de femmes virent jouer ou lurent les pièces de Françoise Pascal? La Roche-Guilhen connaissait-elle le théâtre de Desjardins? [...] il y a peu de chose dans le texte de leurs pièces qui permette aux lecteurs non avertis de les identifier comme des productions féminines. [...] Ceux qui connaissent le théâtre féminin datant de cette même époque en Angleterre, surtout les comédies d'Aphra Behn, risquent d'être déçus par cette absence presque totale de revendications féministes.*

> (Even in the period 1650 to 1750, where we find a considerable number of women authors who managed to get their plays performed by professional actors and to get them published during their own lifetime, it is difficult to see much interaction. For example, how many women saw performances of or read Françoise Pascal? Was La Roche-Guilhen familiar with Mlle Desjardins' theatre? There is little in the texts of their plays which would be recognised as feminist by the unenlightened reader [...] Those who know English women's theatre in this period, and particularly Aphra Behn's comedies might easily be disappointed by the almost total absence of feminist claims.)[33]

The question of cross-influence between French and English women's theatre in the second half of the seventeenth century is no less vexed. In the preface to *An Evening's Love*, Dryden insisted that foreign borrowings had always to be much heightened for the English stage 'which is incomparably more curious in all the ornaments of dramatic poesy than the French or the Spanish'.[34] Much of the fierce defence of English independence in *An Essay of Dramatic Poesy* might be used to keep Mrs Behn apart from Mrs de Villedieu. Dryden writes:

> For if you consider the plots, our own are fuller of variety; if the writing ours are more quick and fuller of spirit; and therefore 'tis a

32. See H. C. Lancaster, *A History of French Dramatic Literature in the Seventeenth-Century,* (Baltimore, John Hopkins Press, 1929–42), III, p.544.

33. See *Les Femmes dramaturges,* p.17.

34. *Dryden: a Selection,* ed. J. Conaghan, (London: Methuen and Co., 1978), p.543.

strange mistake in those who decry the way of writing plays in verse, as if the English therein imitated the French. We have borrowed nothing from them; our plots are weaved in English looms. We endeavour therein to follow the variety and the greatness of characters which are derived to us from Shakespeare and Fletcher; the copiousness and well-knitting of the intrigues we have from Jonson; and for the verse itself we have English precedents of elder date than any of Corneille's plays [...][35]

Mme de Villedieu's plays, like the majority of French plays after Corneille, and unlike so many of her novels, which were immediately made English, were not translated. Nor is there any record of their having been performed in England. While reading them in the original — or in the form of reports of the Parisian and court performances — would not, as we have seen, have presented a problem for the bilingual Mrs Behn, had she found them of interest, it would, of course, have made the texts more difficult to obtain. Ultimately the closest connection between these two women's writings may come through their bitter experience of love, as expressed in their personal letters. Mme de Villedieu's may be seen as a compelling real-life version of the *Lettres portugaises*, one of the recognised sources of inspiration for Aphra Behn's epistolary fiction.

It is fair to conclude that these two parallel theatrical lives meet only in infinity. The fact that plays after Corneille did not cross the channel as easily as novels, particularly when the author was a woman, left both Mme de Villedieu and her English double to struggle on separately against the same prejudices and problems. One may assume that the absence of any feeling of solidarity with women dramatists in other parts of Europe was a factor making their progress in the theatre more difficult. Curiously enough, the next play by a French woman was indeed performed at the English court by order of the francophile monarch Charles II in 1677: the aptly entitled *Rare-en-Tout*, a comedy-ballet by Anne de La Roche-Guilhen (author of numerous fairy-tales, then in the service of the Duchess of Grafton), wife of Henry Fitzroy, the King's illegitimate son. By the only account that remains of it, this play, personifying Europe and the Thames as a pair of singing nymph-like creatures, was 'a lamentable, ill-acted French play' that did little to advance the cause of either French women's drama or French opera in England.[36] But then Mlle de La Roche-Guilhen did not have Mme de Villedieu's unique experience of working with Molière on a command performance at Versailles.

35. Ibid., p.516.
36. See *Les Femmes dramaturges*, p.136.

French Romanticism & the Actresses

Christopher Smith

Since the late sixteenth century, the time of the much admired Isabella Andreini,[1] actresses have, as Jan Clarke reminds us, been a potent force on the French stage: where Marie Champmeslé had led in the seventeenth century, Adrienne Lecouvreur followed in the eighteenth.[2] Given the notorious evanescence of acting, it is always difficult to determine precisely what it was in her playing of, for instance, Houdar de la Motte's powerful *Inès de Castro* that led contemporary commentators to eulogise this not-especially good-looking actress's unusual degree of naturalness in performance. All the same, the implied comparisons are clear enough here, just as they are in remarks about her concern to select costumes particularly suited to the role she was playing. Not for her an all-purpose grand manner, nor a fashionable court dress. Exactly what it was that inspired her to opt for something else is by no means clear.

The temptation, however, is to wonder whether one factor might not have been the truncation of her training, which, paradoxically, may have been to her advantage. She is said to have made her mark first as Pauline in Corneille's *Polyeucte* at the tender age of thirteen. But it is by no means certain that the *Soeurs de l'Instruction chrétienne*, who were responsible for her education, would have been able to do much more to form her celebrated acting style than they had to develop her notoriously fragile moral sensibility. Though she later became a pupil of Marc-Antoine Le Grand at the Comédie-Française, the necessity of making money (she made her professional début, not in Paris, but in Lille when she was only fifteen), and then pregnancy, interrupted his instruction. Her triumph in Crébillon's *Électre* in 1717 and a thousand performances in the next thirteen years — in comedy as well as tragedy — in a hundred roles, including no fewer than twenty-two premières, bespeak great quickness of talent. Yet it is hard to avoid all suspicion that naturalness was perhaps at a premium when deeply considered interpretations were hardly feasible.

In France the latter part of the eighteenth century was a period of considerable debate about the state of the theatrical establishment. The chequered subsequent history of the Odéon should not lead to any underestimate of the significance of efforts to bring into being a second Théâtre-Français,[3] and in 1786 Jean-Henri Dugazon founded what he called the École Royale de Déclamation.[4] It would perhaps be wrong to make too much play with the name of the institution, which was later to become the Conservatoire, were it not that there is abundant reason for thinking that it lived up to it. Dugazon was a Marseillais (which arouses some apprehensions about his natural pronunciation) and an actor whose success had come

1. P. Matthieu, *Histoire de France [...] du règne de Henri IV*, 2 vols (Paris: Métayer et Guillemot,1605), II, p.209ff, and I. Du Ryer, *Le Temps perdu* (Paris: du Bray, 1610), pp.65-66.
2. P. Germain, *Adrienne Lecouvreur, tragédienne* (Paris: Lanore, 1983): see, too, my entry for Adrienne Lecouvreur in *An Encyclopedia of Continental Women Writers*, ed. K. M.Wilson, 2 vols (New York: Garland, 1991).
3. P. Morel and G. Monval, *L'Odéon: histoire [...] du second Théâtre français* (Paris: Lemerre, 1876).
4. H. F. Collins, *Talma: A Biography of an Actor* (London: Faber, 1964), pp. 28-29: see, too, Roman d'Amat's notice on Dugazon in the *Dictionnnaire de biographie française*.

predominantly in comic roles, which makes his pedagogical predilections somewhat surprising. All the same, the fact remains that the training he provided was above all, in the speaking of the classical alexandrine, in the grand manner. Lekain (for Voltaire), followed — admittedly at a distance — by Brizzard (for Jean-François Ducis), moved only cautiously as they experimented with departures from traditional acting styles, and though Garrick was admired on his visits to Paris in the 1760s,[5] his direct influence on stage performance was limited.

If one figure above all has to be identified as the harbinger of change it must be François-Joseph Talma.[6] Coming in his teens from London, where his father practised as a fashionable dentist, he entered the *École Royale de Déclamation*. There is no need to sketch out his career here: neither his embracing of Republican principles and subsequent elevation to the questionable privilege of being Napoleon's favourite actor, nor his readiness to adopt what he fondly believed to be historically accurate costume, leading him to appear bare-legged as Proclus in Voltaire's *Brutus* in January 1789. For present purposes it will be more revealing to turn to Ducis's *Othello*.[7] In its first production, we can see, if we pause to look into it at some detail, further evidence of the different ways in which actors and actresses responded to the challenge of breaking with a grand tradition which was threatening to become mere theatrical routine. The readiness of the actresses to accept innovation may well be as much a result of the scantiness of their training as of the fieriness of their temperament.

There can be little doubt that it was Talma, the driving force at what was then called the Théâtre de la République,[8] who persuaded Ducis to add *Othello* in 1792 to the series of Shakespeare adaptations he had inaugurated as far back as 1769 with his *Hamlet*, with Brizzard in the lead. Resident in Versailles, Ducis had at first welcomed the Revolution and was keen to play his part in the evolution of new political institutions. Being intelligent as well as sensitive, he was, however, soon alarmed by the violent turn of events that would lead, not to the constitutional monarchy for which he longed, but to the Terror. Loss of pensions and patronage obliged Ducis to look for income, but he was resolved to keep a low profile. He would most likely have done so if Talma had not persuaded him to come out of retirement and provide him with an impressive role. This was just one more phase in a

Adrienne Lecouvreur

5. G. W. Stone Jr and G. M. Kahrl, *David Garrick: A Criticial Biography* (Carbondale: South Illinois University Press, 1979),esp. pp.293-312.

6. Collins, *Talma*; A. Copin, *Talma et la Révolution* (Paris: Frinzine, 1887); *Talma et l'Empire*, 2nd ed. (Paris: Frinzine, 1888); and C. Talma, *Études sur l'art théâtral, suivies d'anecdotes inédites sur Talma et de la correspondance de Ducis avec cet artiste* (Paris: Feret, 1836).

7. J.-F. Ducis, *Othello*, ed. Christopher Smith, [Textes littéraires No.80] (Exeter University Press, 1991). See, too, J. Golder, *Shakespeare for the Age of Reason: the earliest stage adaptations of Jean-François Ducis, 1769-1792*, [Studies in Shakespeare and the Eighteenth Century, No. 295] (Oxford: Voltaire Foundation, 1992).

8. M. Carlson, *The Theatre of the French Revolution* (Ithaca, NY: Cornell UP, 1966).

long association in the course of which Ducis had been prepared to adapt and alter for Talma both his own texts and those of such dramatists as Voltaire. The significance of this is that we have here proof that the playwright was prepared to be accommodating to a fine actor with a forceful personality.

This French *Othello* should not be regarded as a translation of Shakespeare's tragedy, which Ducis could not in fact even read in the original. It is an adaptation designed to make it conform largely to French Classical dramaturgy and a reinterpretation of the story in terms of late-eighteenth-century sensibility. Three points reveal something quite important about the differences between what actors and actresses were prepared to do on stage at this time.

In Act V in the original version (though not in the alternative happy ending), Othello kills Hédelmone, as Desdemona has become. How? Not with the homely Shakespearean pillow, which disappears — like the notorious handkerchief — earlier in the play, but with an elegant, nobler, probably oriental, dagger.[9] Then there is the question of Othello's skin colour. In his *Avertissement*, Ducis declares that he knows perfectly well that in London actors playing Othello blacken their faces, but he argues that following their example would not please the Parisian audiences, especially not the ladies. Accordingly, he has not given his hero a black face, but one which is yellow and copper coloured, *'jaune et cuivré'*. This, he observes, would not be out of character for someone from the African coast and would moreover make it easier for everyone to appreciate the facial expressions of the actor taking the role.

This is all very well, but we have here a departure from what not only Ducis, but also his public in 1792 knew as a famous feature of the original. The playwright says that he made the decisions about this, and that may be true. Even if it is, however, there must be significance in the fact that Talma did not protest, for he had a strong personality and, as we have seen, often struck out against convention in such matters as costume. So it might be thought more probable that Talma preferred to perform his role in light make-up, even if he did not actually suggest it should be. In other words, whether because of a desire not to invite the ridicule with which the Parisian public invariably greeted any departure from norms, particularly where Shakespeare was involved, or out of a genuine concern not to imperil the creation of an impressive heroic stage image, Talma drew back from this particular challenge. Who exactly proposed that we may never know, but we are entitled to be confident that Ducis would not, and indeed could not, have resisted if Talma had insisted on a black-faced Othello. Could we have in this one of the reasons why before the first performance of Ducis's *Othello*, Talma was, as Carbon des Flins des Oliviers recorded in the *Journal de Paris*, 'worried about the innovations that the French poet, following the English one, has introduced into our drama'?[10]

But what of Hédelmone in Act V? Referring yet again to the prefatory *Avertissement*, we find Ducis stating that the 'Willow Song' is something he just would not dream of giving up. It would appear to be logical to wonder whether or not this gives some indication

9. Oriental weaponry adds local colour to Voltaire's *Zadig*.

10. Quoted by M. Gilman, *Othello in French*, [Bibliothèque de la Revue de Littérature comparée] (Paris: Champion), pp.57-58.

that he (perhaps under pressure from others) had been contemplating doing just that. Chérubin's *romance* in the second act of *Le Mariage de Figaro* had been regarded as a striking innovation. Introducing song on the tragic stage was, however, altogether more daring. That the 'Willow Song' was a feature of Shakespeare's play, well-known in eighteenth-century France, is certainly clear enough, yet we have already seen what happened to two other striking features, and the adaptation by Ducis, whatever else may be said about it, is in general anything but slavish. Plainly, the crucial feature was performance, and here we may see an actress coming to the rescue of what we may call a proto-Romantic development on the French stage.

Magdelaine-Marie — or Louise, or else (following fashions of stage pseudonymity) Juliette — Desgarcins, in her early twenties (and so distinctly younger than Talma) at the time of the première of *Othello*, had received some training from Fleury, Dugazon and Molé.[11] None the less, she risked breaking all convention by singing on the tragic stage, and this won her gratitude from Ducis. Some idea of the lengths he was prepared to go to in order to retain the 'Willow Song' emerges when we recall that the playwright cast his '*Romance du Saule*' in the same verse form as the one used as early as 1776 by Le Tourneur in his translation of *Othello*,[12] and for which an attractive melody had been provided by Paul-Égide Martin, the composer best-known nowadays for the song *Plaisir d'amour*. This suggests fairly clearly that the original intention of Ducis was to have his words sung to Martin's tune. But this apparently proved too demanding, probably because of its awkward *tessitura*, for Mademoiselle Desgarcins. The solution was to ask the popular composer André-Ernest-Modeste Grétry to write a new melody that demanded rather less of the singer.[13]

With Grétry's setting of the '*Romance du Saule*' Mademoiselle Desgarcins created a great impression in the theatre, remarkable no less for her courage than for the aesthetic appeal of her performance. What we have here, then, is not simply evidence of the readiness of Ducis to go to considerable lengths in order to preserve what he calls on of the 'features' of the play he was adapting, but also grounds for thinking that it would be odd if others had been sacrificed unless special pressure had been applied. Furthermore, though playing Othello was a landmark in Talma's career, it was his Hédelmone who emerged as the more progressive performer, which undermines to some degree Talma's status as the great innovative actor of his time. Whether Mademoiselle Desgarcins was really more daring, or else emerged more readily brow-beaten into taking a risk, it would be hard to determine. But again we may see evidence that it was the actress who was more flexible, perhaps less inhibited by temperament and less hide-bound by training and convention than her male counterpart.

Developments in real life rarely follow straight-forward patterns, and Romanticism was, as everyone knows, slow in its evolution in France. Any speculation we can make as to whether Mademoiselle Desgarcins might have continued in the same direction is cut short by her death in 1797, though she did have time to appear in a new

11. M. Pollitzer, *Le Premier Amour de Talma: Mademoiselle Desgarcins (1769-1797)* (Paris: Nouvelles Éditions latines, 1951).

12. Le Tourneur, *Shakespeare, traduit de l'anglois*, 20 vols (Paris: 1776-83), I.

13. D. Charlton, *Grétry and the Growth of Opéra-comique* (CUP, 1986).

production of *Roi Léar* by Ducis. Napoleon, perhaps in order to silence subversive chatter about lowly Corsican origins, made the revival of French Classicism an instrument of Imperial policy, and if he enjoyed Talma in the *Macbeth* of Ducis, it was in the classical role of Cinna that he presented him before an audience of monarchs at Erfurt. Comparisons with Girolamo Crescentini, the Emperor's favourite *castrato*, of whom Vigny presents a scathing portrait in *Servitude et grandeur militaires*,[14] should not be pushed very far, but they are not without some validity. Before Talma died in 1826 there were at last signs of change, and after his death Romantic writers made something of a cult of him as the acting profession's lost leader.[15] However, had he lived on, he would have been elderly for the lead in the dramas of Hugo and Dumas. The melodramas of Guilbert de Pixérécourt were an important element in the evolution that was taking place, but the emphasis in them is on texture and stage setting, and though children — even dogs — are allotted enhanced roles, actresses are not given especially significant parts, sometimes virtually none at all.[16]

Before considering the next phase in the evolution of female acting in the French theatre, we should, however, recognise the part played by Harriet Smithson.[17] An Irish actress, born in the first year of the century, she made little impact when she essayed the step up from Crow Street, Dublin, to Drury Lane. However, in crossing the Channel in 1828 with William Macready, and again in 1832, she had sensational successes in Paris at the Odéon as Desdemona (that play again!), Ophelia and Juliet, then as Jane Shore in Nicholas Rowe's tragedy, and as Virginia in that by Sheridan Knowles. Only one of those four was modern, and even then in classicising vein, but Stendhal and Berlioz in their different ways were to bear witness to her power to stir Romantic passions. There are hints that she emphasised her points with particular vigour in order to put them across to a public not entirely at home with the language in which she performed, and the fact that she and her companions were better received than an earlier touring troupe half a decade earlier, might be taken as justification of her artistic policy, even if allowances must be made too for changes in the political and artistic climate.[18] However that may be, there can be little doubt that it was in particular the wholehearted acting of Henrietta Smithson that opened the eyes of a new generation of French playwrights to fresh opportunities in the theatre.

The impact might have been more marked still, but for a quirk of Victor Hugo's literary imagination. His private life might well have been supposed to have equipped him to an exceptional degree with varied passionate personal experiences that might well have been conducive to a quite exceptional portrayal of womankind.[19] Instead, however, his female characters are, for the most part, stereotypes, and in the case of the younger ones in particular, rather dull ones at that.[20] In *Hernani*, to take the most obvious first example, if the role of the eponymous hero offered Firmin intriguing possibilities in the apparently contradictory role of a Hamletic bandit, that of the philandering king who is transmuted into a sage emperor

14. A. de Vigny, *Servitude et grandeur militaires*, ed. J.Cruickshank, [Textes classiques et modernes] (University of London Press, 1966), p.194, and the note on p.249, where Crescentini is coyly categorised as a counter-tenor.

15. See, for example, Alexandre Dumas père, *Mémoires de J.-F. Talma*, 4 vols (Paris: Souverain, 1850).

16. W. G. Hartog, *Guilbert de Pixérécourt* (Paris: Champion, 1913).

17. P. Raby, *'Fair Ophelia': A Life of Harriet Smithson Berlioz* (CUP, 1982).

18. F.W.J. Hemmings, *The Theatre Industry in France* (CUP), pp.84–85.

19. H. Guillemin, *Hugo et la sexualité* (Paris: Gallimard, 1954).

20. For detailed information about the casts for the French Romantic plays, see M. Descotes, *Le Drame romantique et ses grand créateurs* (Paris: PUF, 1955). W.D. Howarth, in *Sublime and Grotesque* (London: Harrap, 1975), surveys the entire field of French Romantic drama, always keeping theatrical considerations in mind.

after contemplating his destiny in the vaults was no less demanding on Michelot, and Joanny plainly saw the possibilities of converting the potentially comical Don Ruy Gomez into a menacing figure of tragic dignity. But for the most part, Mademoiselle Mars, who had herself been a notable Chérubin a quarter of a century earlier in 1802[21] and was now getting on for fifty, needed only to be statuesquely beautiful as Doña Sol. Only in the last act did she have the opportunity of moving from an essentially decorative part to one that has something of the inner contradictions required in Romantic drama, and it is by no means certain she thoroughly relished the opportunity. There are the beginnings here, to be sure, but nothing like full development.

'Purity, dignity and pathos', these are the qualities that Hugo lauded in Mademoiselle Louise Baudoin, the actress playing the queen in *Ruy Blas*. This may be contrasted with the performance of the actor who, in words by Hugo that seem almost designed to strengthen the hypothesis about the inadequacies of conventionally trained performers being advanced here, passed through a whole gamut of emotions to soar to tragic heights at the end. To the older generation, he was 'Lekain and Garrick' incarnate in a single actor, and contemporaries recognised in him the physical energy of Kean and the emotionality of Talma. Who was he? None other than Frédéric Lemaître.[22] Despite the kind things Hugo says about the actors at the *Comédie-Française*, he had appreciated that for his Romantic drama to reach its full height it needed to quit that tradition-bound institution and look to the Boulevard where melodrama had flourished and absorbed — partly through German influence — a very large amount of the Romantic spirit.

And now it is the turn of another actress to come into the limelight: she is, of course, Marie Dorval.[23] The details of her private life can well remain private, for if there is truth in the statements by some biographers that her life was no less stormy than the parts that she played, there were, conversely, many who had stormy lives who either never trod the boards or else (as we shall be reminded by and by) played demure roles. What is significant for our purposes, however, is the fact that she, like Adrienne Lecouvreur, had only a truncated training, and whether even that had much influence on a style of performance bred of abundant practical experience on provincial stages going back to her earliest childhood has to be questioned. It seems most likely that all she would have learned was something about voice production, for certainly when she came to the notice of the Parisian public by playing at the *Théâtre Porte-Saint-Martin* it was not classical restraint and grandeur — not '*stille Größe*' — that made an impression nor minutely observed interpretation of comic roles from the classical repertory. No, it was rather her strength and passion, her total identification with her roles in a physical style that was felt to be unrestrained by comparison with what was admired at the *Comédie-Française* as skilled and tasteful acting. In *Antony*, a sequel to her 1827 triumph in the far less literary *Trente ans dans la vie d'un joueur* by Ducange, she had a huge success. Not surprisingly, Hugo also entrusted her with the

21. M. Descotes, *Les Grands Rôles dans le théâtre de Beaumarchais* (Paris: PUF, 1974), p.228.
22. R. Baldick, *The Life and Times of Frédérick Lemaître* (London: Hamish Hamilton, 1959). Hugo's appreciation of the actor is quoted on p.169.
23. P. Hagenauer, *La Vie douloureuse de Marie Dorval* (Paris: 1972); F.Moser, *Marie Dorval* (Paris: 1947). See, too, my entry on Marie Dorval in *An Encyclopedia of Continental Women Writers*.

part of the heroine in his *Marion Delorme*. By all accounts it was the *subject* of the *Dix ans, ou La Vie d'une femme*, not her interpretation of its lead, which caused the public to be less satisfied with her roles in Scribe's play, though one might have thought that Parisian audiences were becoming familiar with sympathetic plays about fallen women by this time. However that may be, she moved on next, in what might be thought an astonishing tribute to her gifts, to the *Comédie-Française*.

There she played Catarina in Hugo's *Angelo*, sparking off, it is said, a remarkable performance from Mademoiselle Mars (playing opposite as La Tisbé) as the two actresses, for reasons that hardly call for investigation, conceived a hearty distaste for one another. Her best was, however, yet to come.

In Alfred de Vigny's *Chatterton*, a play set in the London of the late eighteenth century, hers was the role of Kitty, the young and sensitive wife of a hard-faced Englishman. The part demanded a mixture of timidity and passion bordering on hysteria. The conclusion was the most spectacular of all the fainting fits that feature in so many Romantic works to symbolise the victory of feeling over reason and the primacy of the emotional over the corporeal. Not for her a fit of the vapours (Beaumarchais's Suzanne, it will be recalled, remarked with impertinent pertinency that that was a complaint that afflicted only upper-class females), nor a sudden slumping to the ground. Instead, Marie Dorval emerged from the bedroom where young Chatterton lay dead, collapsed on the landing, slid down stairs and ended up in a crumpled heap at their foot as a fine tornado curtain fell on the scene.

Bannister sliding has unfortunately acquired too many connotations of *Just William*, but here we have, from the notoriously impermanent art of acting, an emblem of what a woman like Marie Dorval could bring to the *Comédie-Française*.

Subsequent events show how unpalatable that grand old institution found it. A great theatrical success was one thing, but acceptance by the *sociétaires* of such goings-on was another. Shortly after *Chatterton*, Marie Dorval left the *Comédie-Française*, and though she did return briefly to star in George Sand's utterly unsuccessful *Cosima*, it was back at the *Théâtre Porte-Saint Martin* that she had her last great role as the heroine of the highly popular (in every sense) *Marie-Jeanne, ou La Fille du peuple*, by Dennery and Mallian.

It would satisfy a certain criterion of tidy straight-forwardness if we could now move on smartly to Sarah Bernhardt. But life, and the theatre which imitates life, is not like that, and we cannot leave unaccounted the part played in the development of drama by Rachel.[24] Beauty is in the eye of the beholder; in this case, Jules Janin's, the drama critic of the *Journal des Débats*. He was attracted by her looks and talents when she made her *début* at the Gymnase, having been rescued from a career of singing for pennies in the street by the impressario Choron. Both her background and the early influences on her career pointed to something not unlike Marie Dorval's experiences. But her training, albeit received rather late from Samson, proved highly efficacious. She did, it is true, succeed

24. B. Falk, *Rachel the Immortal* (London: Hutchinson, 1935).

in melodramatic roles, including that of Adrienne Lecouvreur in Scribe's dramatisation of the famous actress's life, but her real triumphs came rather in the classics and, more interestingly, in what we can accurately call the neo-Classical dramas of Ponsard.[25] The tempatation is to see all this as breaking the pattern. It might well, however, be more accurate to think in terms of a Classicism that was all the more potent, just as it had been in the Baroque age, since audiences could be aware of the passion beneath the polish, the personality beneath the performance, and the force that was being held in check to reinvigorate the conventional form.

From here, we can take the step to Sarah Bernhardt, with a range as astonishingly wide as her personal experience that was commensurate with the length of her prodigious career.[26] Again, we note the stormy relationship with the *Comédie-Française*, and to that we can add a phenomenon that is worth separate investigation, the growing tendency of French actresses to run their own theatrical companies. To her, the classics (think of her Phèdre on an early gramophone record) and Romanticism (her Doña Sol) came both alike. Perhaps even more strikingly, she could breathe something like life and authenticity into the contrived and prosaic melodramas of Sardou, something that we can only experience nowadays when the plots and passions are conveyed through the intoxicating medium of Puccini's music. She essayed Shakespeare, passing on from Cordelia and Juliet to a remarkable Hamlet. A summation of her skill and versatility comes with her playing the lead in *L'Aiglon*, a play which, like Edmond Rostand's *Cyrano de Bergerac*, may well be seen as a late flowering of Romanticism.[27]

What conclusions can we advance? First should be the significance of the role of actresses in the development of French acting styles in the Romantic period and after. Along with this goes some loosening of the shackles of tradition in a culture that tended to be hide-bound for reasons not unconnected with the problems of a quasi-autonomous corporation of players under state control in a nineteenth century which brought many changes of regime. There is ample evidence of the inferior educational and training opportunities open to actresses at the time. This could well guide us into those familiar questions of nature and nurture, which once bedeviled discussions of poetic ability and have now taken on a fresh lease of life in the feminist debates moved by the likes of de Beauvoir. It seems impossible to discount the pressures — both societal and economic — that both led to and resulted in the actresses' complex and, in nearly all cases, fraught personal lives, conducing career breaks through pregnancies and various illnesses, whether physical or pschyosomatic. Yet despite all this actresses made their distinctive contribution to the emergence of Romanticism on the French stage. That they did it against the odds is all the more to their credit. The next phase of the development belongs to the history of the cinema, but that is another story.

25. W.D. Howarth, 'Neo-Classicism in France: a re-assessment', in *Studies in the French Eighteenth Century presented to John Lough*, ed. D.J. Mossop et al. (University of Durham Press, 1978), pp.92-107 (esp. pp.98-107). The term 'neo-Classical' is so fraught with difficulties that it is tempting to seek another to highlight trends in the late eighteenth century and early in the next. Greek Revival, though familiar to art historians, is rather too restrictive as it allows far too little for the revival of interests in Roman styles in the same period.

26. S. Bernhardt *My Double Life* (London, Heinemann, 1907).

27. Howarth, *Sublime and Grotesque*, pp. 386-98.

Reform of the German Theatre: Frau Neuber & Frau Gottsched

Lesley Sharpe

Lesley Sharpe is Senior Lecturer in German at the University of Exeter

In the first half of the eighteenth century, two women made a major contribution to the renaissance of the German theatre. Both were allies of the dominant literary arbiter of the 1730s and 40s, Johann Christoph Gottsched, but both were superior to him in imagination and literary talent. The first was the *Prinzipalin* (actress-manageress) Caroline Neuber, whose work was vital in creating the conditions for the emergence of a theatre of literary value; the second was Gottsched's wife, Luise Adelgunde Viktoria, whose translations and original comedies pointed the way towards a high German comedy. The lasting benefits of Gottsched's attempts to bring literary drama and the stage together were due in a significant degree to the talented help he received from these two women, but Gottsched's relationship to both of them was problematic. He recognised their talents and their value to him, but he always put their interests second to his own.

Caroline Neuber was born Caroline Weissenborn in 1697 in Zwickau, Saxony, the daughter of an influential lawyer. Always of a violent temper, he became increasingly tyrannical as gout made him more and more of an invalid. The young Caroline's mother had died when she was seven years old, and the intolerable circumstances at home made the energetic and well-educated girl determined to escape. One attempt at flight with a young associate of her father whom she wished to marry ended by their both being brought back to Erfurt on an open cart and threatened with imprisonment. Eventually, in 1717, she did flee, literally having to scale the garden wall of her home. With her fiancé — later her husband — Johann Neuber, she joined the Spiegelberg troupe of actors and her career began.[1]

There were in Germany at the time three main spheres of theatrical activity.[2] First, there were the court theatres, which of course were numerous in an Empire consisting of over three hundred separate states. To a limited extent these catered also for a non-court audience. The court theatres specialised in Italian opera and in French plays put on by French players, as French was the language spoken at most of the courts. Secondly, there was the amateur theatre. In the seventeenth century there was a lively tradition of school drama — plays written for and put on by Protestant and Catholic boys' schools. School drama had disappeared by the end of the seventeenth century, but the lively participation (for example among the country aristocracy) in amateur theatricals was its legacy. The third sphere was the so-called *Wanderbühne* — the travelling

1. The fullest account of Frau Neuber's career, using and reproducing original letters that show the extent of her intelligence and education, is still that of Friedrich von Reden-Esbeck, *Caroline Neuber und ihre Zeitgenossen. Ein Beitrag zur deutschen Kultur und Theatergeschichte*, Leipzig, 1881. A concise and yet comparatively detailed account is in B. Becker-Cantarino, *Der lange Weg zur Mündigkeit. Frauen und Literatur in Deutschland von 1500 bis 1800* (Munich, 1989), pp.310-317.

2. The most detailed and useful account in English of the German theatre in this period is still W.H. Bruford, *Theatre, Drama and Audience in Goethe's Germany* (London, 1950), in particular pp. 1-85. For a concise overview of troupes and their main locations, see H.A. Frenzel, *Geschichte des Theaters. Daten und Dokumente 1470-1890*, 2nd edition (Munich, 1984), pp.228-272.

companies who specialised in extemporised theatre of two kinds in particular: the historical costume drama, known as the *Haupt- und Staatsaktion*, and farce, in which an important part was played by the traditional German comic person, Hanswurst, a kind of German equivalent to Harlequin. So popular was Hanswurst that he even interrupted the *Haupt- und Staatsaktion* with farcical interludes. The *Wanderbühne* often had a very difficult time making ends meet, even if a company won the principal rights to perform in a particular state or city. Outside of Vienna there were virtually no permanent, purpose-built houses for the commercial theatre. The Neubers had to improvise structures in many odd places. In spite of such practical obstacles there were often long traditions in the families of the travelling companies. The Spiegelberg troupe, which the Neubers first joined, was led by a former member of the Velten company, which had been formed in the 1670s. The Neubers then trained mostly with the Haack-Hofmann company, the continuation of the Velten company. In 1727 they founded their own, which in turn formed the training ground for some of the great actor-managers to come, notably Johann Friedrich Schönemann, with whose troupe Ackermann and Sophie Schröder trained, and Heinrich Gottfried Koch, with whom Eckhof worked. The influence of French and English troupes in Germany led to the slow introduction of actresses during the seventeenth century, so that by the time Frau Neuber began her career they were well established within the companies.

In 1727 the Neubers were approached by the Leipzig professor Johann Christoph Gottsched, who hoped to find a sympathetic company to further his aims for the development of the German theatre. Gottsched wished to use the theatre as a channel of popular moral education and enlightenment. He wished also to improve its status culturally so that Germany, like Britain and France, would develop a theatrical tradition of European stature. He was only one of many Germans at the time who lamented the lack of a living German theatrical tradition that would give rise to works of literary merit, but he had the energy to see the project through. He also enjoyed the backing of the membership of the Leipzig German Society, a society of scholars and professional men who similarly espoused the aim of making the German language and German letters internationally respected.[3]

Gottsched found the Neubers ready to accommodate at least some of his suggestions. Frau Neuber had, before meeting Gottsched, already begun to try to use fixed texts rather than working exclusively from scenarios and extemporisation. She put the troupe to work to memorise not only prose plays but also verse plays. She also tried to accommodate Gottsched's pedantic attitude towards verisimilitude in the design of costumes. Part of the appeal of the old *Haupt- und Staatsaktion* was the element of spectacle. The grand costumes in particular defied any notion of historical authenticity. She also encouraged a greater naturalness of style in acting: gesture and delivery, often exaggerated, became more restrained. Fixed texts also meant the development of ensemble playing rather than reliance on virtuoso performances by individuals. In fact Eduard Devrient,

3. For a recent concise account of Gottsched's reforms see F.J. Lamport, *German Classical Drama. Theatre, Humanity and Nation 1750-1870* (Cambridge, 1990), pp.7-13.

WOMEN IN EUROPEAN THEATRE

one of the first historians of the German theatre and a member of an old theatrical family, credited Frau Neuber with founding the first German school of acting.[4]

It was clear that Frau Neuber saw in her alliance with Gottsched a means not only of elevating the literary and artistic standing of the theatre but also of raising the status of the acting profession. Needless to say, the rewards for members of travelling companies were very insecure. Actors and actresses were *déclassés*, outside the hierarchy of the corporate society. In addition, actresses had a highly dubious moral reputation, and in the court theatres certainly did provide a source of mistresses for the aristocracy. Frau Neuber tried to improve the reputation of the profession. Unmarried actresses lived with her and were strictly supervised. By the last decades of the eighteenth century actresses were held in considerably higher regard.

One of the practical problems connected with Gottsched's theatrical reforms was the lack of actable, stageworthy plays. He therefore encouraged his students and adherents to translate and thus create a new repertoire, chiefly drawn from the French classical stage. Corneille's *Cinna* and *Le Cid* were performed, also Racine's *Iphigénie* and *Bérénice*, as well as a popular adaptation of Corneille's *Horace*, entitled *Die Horazier*, by a Hamburg merchant named Behrmann. There was also Gottsched's own play *Der sterbende Cato* (*Dying Cato*), but the native German repertoire was very small and even less popular than serious French plays in translation. In the early 1730s the Neuber company began to perform French comedies in translation. Soon, comedy performances were outnumbering tragedies by three to one. It may well have been an initiative of Frau Neuber that brought so many comedies on to the stage. Koch, one of her talented young actors, was a speedy and able translator. Frau Neuber always retained a strong sense of the practical in spite of her support of reform. She knew that audiences could take only so much of this highly literary theatre. Gottsched himself was pleased with the success of French comedies in translation — Molière and Destouches were the most popular. No doubt the dominant satirical tendency in them satisfied his moralistic and didactic view of art and the theatre. These stage successes were also a reason why he set his own wife the task of writing and translating comedies.

Financial survival continued to be a struggle for Frau Neuber. In the most important symbolic act of her career, she solemnly banished Hanswurst from the stage in a short prelude performed in 1737.[5] This action represented the commitment of her troupe to a higher ideal of theatre as elevated entertainment. As a gesture it attracted scepticism and ridicule; nevertheless, it has been seen subsequently as a turning point in the development of German comedy. However one views the gesture, it was a brave and risky move, for the public loved Hanswurst and her great rival at the time in Leipzig, J. F. Müller, the man who had succeeded in wresting from her the Saxon *Privilegium*, was a virtuoso Hanswurst. Yet the comic figure was not banished in reality from her stage, but reappeared in toned-down guises, so the banishment was a banishment in name only.[6] Frau Neuber was too shrewd and realistic

4. *Geschichte der deutschen Schauspielkunst*, revised edition by W. Stuhlfeldt (Berlin/Zurich, 1929), p.99. Devrient gives a useful account of the history of the Neuber company.

5. On the Hanswurst figure see H. G. Asper, *Hanswurst. Studien zum Lustigmacher auf der Berufsschauspielerbühne in Deutschland im 17. und 18. Jahrhundert* (Emsdetten, 1980). On the changing expectations of audiences with regard to comedy see John Walter van Cleve, *Harlequin Besieged. The Reception of Comedy in Germany during the Early Enlightenment* (Berne, Frankfurt, Las Vegas, 1980).

6. As Lessing points out in his *Hamburgische Dramaturgie*, Achtzehntes Stück (Stuttgart, 1981), pp.97–98.

to think she could manage without one of the mainstays of the theatre's popularity, and in spite of her support for regular drama always retained a mixed bill.

It was this conflict between the aims of a theatre with pretensions to literary value and the need to survive that brought about Frau Neuber's break with Gottsched. They quarrelled over the business of staging; Gottsched insisted on greater authenticity of costume and set than she felt the audience would accept or she could deliver. In addition Gottsched was determined to press ahead with his project to publish the original German plays that he and his followers had contributed to the new repertoire in a series entitled *Die Deutsche Schaubühne*. He wanted to create an educated public by extending the availability of the plays through the mass medium of the printed word. But for people in the theatre world, learning fixed texts was one thing, having them published was another. In the days when many plays remained unpublished, acting companies jealously guarded 'their' plays and resisted attempts to make them more widely accessible. Gottsched's programme of enlightenment and his aim to create an educated public therefore brought him into conflict with the interests of actual companies in this transitional phase from extemporised to text-based theatre. Frau Neuber herself wrote several plays and numerous short preludes and after-pieces, only one or two of which were ever published, partly for that very reason, but also because they relied on topicality, and because they were a means of expounding the company's aims to the public and so were particular to the Neuber troupe.[7]

Frau Neuber's fortunes declined throughout the 1740s and 50s, though she remained a formidable actress and also retained flexibility and an eye for new talent. She was the first person to stage a play by Lessing, his early comedy *Der junge Gelehrte* (*The Young Scholar*) in 1748. By this time her style was beginning to seem old-fashioned, but this in itself is a mark of how far the theatre had begun to be taken seriously and audiences were developing critical expectations of it. The fascination that the theatre exerted over the next generation of young writers is vividly reflected in Goethe's *Wilhelm Meisters theatralische Sendung* and in the later version, *Wilhelm Meisters Lehrjahre*.

One of the obstacles to reforming the theatre was the lack of actable plays. One of Gottsched's most skilful helpers in trying to overcome this problem was his wife, Luise Adelgunde Viktoria. Born in 1713 in Danzig (now Gdansk), Frau Gottsched came from an academic family and so benefited from a much more extensive education than most girls, even of her station, as girls' education, even among the well-to-do, was often very rudimentary. She had a secure grasp of French and English by the time her correspondence with Gottsched, whom she had met in her parents' house, began in 1729. She had also begun to write poetry. The two married in 1735, and Frau Gottsched, whom her husband often referred to as his 'geschickte Freundin' ('skilful friend') became a dutiful — indispensable — helper to him in his scholarly work and in his various projects in aid of popular enlightenment. She translated large parts of Bayle's

7. Frau Neuber's only extant full-length play is a comedy entitled *Das Schäferfest oder die Herbstfreunde* (The Shepherds' Feast or The Friends of Autumn), dating from 1753 and published in *Deutsche Literatur. Sammlung literarischer Kunst- und Kulturdenkmäler in Entwicklungsreihen. Reihe Aufklärung: Band 3 (Gottscheds Lebens- und Kunstreform)*, ed. F. Brüggemann (Leipzig, 1935).

Dictionary into German, for example, as well as parts of Addison's and Steele's *Spectator*. Her very mature, lucid and intelligent prose style is evident from the beginning of her correspondence with Gottsched, when she was only sixteen, and is especially remarkable when one remembers that she was happier writing in French. Though a keen and able scholar herself, she was always very modest, almost dismissive of her achievements. She did not want to be thought of as a scholar, as though she were competing for attention in a male province, and pointed out to friends that, for her, scholarly work was an enforced substitute for motherhood, which to her regret she never experienced. Apart from her four original comedies and one tragedy, she produced numerous translations which remained for some decades in the repertoire. As a woman playwright she was unusual in the eighteenth century in that most other plays by women were written by women active in the theatre or by aristocratic women for amateur theatricals.[8] In either case their work was almost never published. Though literary historians (looking at published comedy as a literary genre) gave Frau Gottsched the distinction of founding the so-called Saxon comedy, her more vital contribution was arguably in helping to create a theatre-going public with higher expectations, and more research might usefully be done on the afterlife of her comedies as part of the repertoire.[9]

To the modern mind Frau Gottsched seems more than a little put upon by her husband. Gottsched was an advocate of better education for women and of the recognition of their poetic talents. He pressed for the admission of the poet Christina Mariana von Ziegler to the Leipzig German Society as a form of encouragement to female talents. In this he was certainly a great deal more broadminded than many a prominent writer in the later part of the 18th century. Nevertheless, there was no doubt whose work came first in the Gottsched household and Frau Gottsched herself seems to have adopted from her husband a wholly utilitarian view of her creative work, for which she was allowed the time only after she had done the tasks he required.

Frau Gottsched's particular talent was for satirical comedy. All of her work was written under the constraints imposed by her husband; in this instance his idea of comedy. This he set out in his main work of poetics, his *Versuch einer kritischen Dichtkunst vor die Deutschen* (*An Essay in Critical Poetics for the Germans*). Satirical comedy satisfied Gottsched's largely mimetic and didactic view of literature. He demanded that one particular character should be the main object of the audience's laughter. Purely visual comedy was banned. Gottsched demanded a certain degree of realism in speech, commensurate with the fact that comedy was set in a less elevated sphere than tragedy. He insisted that the unities be observed and favoured no more than a ten-hour span for the action. He insisted also on five acts, with an element of mystery or intrigue which should be resolved at the end.

The plots of Frau Gottsched's original comedies, with the exception of her one-act play *Der Witzling* (*The Know-all*), are not really complex enough to sustain a five-act play.[10] Action is rather

8. For a useful survey of women's writing for the theatre see R. P. Dawson, 'Frauen und Theater: Vom Stegreifspiel zum bürgerlichen Rührstück' in *Deutsche Literatur von Frauen*, 1 : *Vom Mittelalter bis zum Ende des 18. Jahrhunderts*, ed. Gisela Brinker-Gabler, (Munich, 1988), pp.421-434.

9. For discussions of Frau Gottsched's work in the context of Saxon comedy and Gottsched's concept of comedy see H. Steinmetz, *Die Komödie der Aufklärung*, Stuttgart, 1966, pp.17-36; Eckehart Catholy, *Das deutsche Lustspiel von der Aufklärung bis zur Romantik* (Stuttgart, Berlin, Cologne, Mainz, 1982), pp.20-33.

10. The most detailed study of Frau Gottsched's work with discussions of her original plays is Victoria Richel's *Luise Gottsched. A Reconsideration* (Berne, 1973).

slight and as a result the main interest lies in a sequence of comic encounters that serve the satirical purpose. *Die Hausfranzösinn* (*The French Housekeeper*) makes fun of the German passion for all things French — and as residents of Leipzig, which was nicknamed 'Little Paris' in the 18th century, the Gottscheds had ample opportunity to see such influence. In particular Frau Gottsched ridicules this Francophilia among the solid middle classes, who should have more sense. She uses stereotypical figures — the worthy but foolish German father with the vain, affected, and (as it transpires) deceitful French employees who lord it over the family. In *Die ungleiche Heirath* (*The Unequal Marriage*) she makes fun of a family of immensely status-conscious but completely impoverished country aristocrats, who try to marry their daughter to a wealthy commoner in order to make him pay off their debts — a plot modelled on Molière's *George Dandin*. In *Das Testament* (*The Will*) she satirises the greed of a brother and sister, and niece and nephew, of a rich widow whose money they are trying to secure. The wealthy lady confounds her relatives in the end by marrying again. The plots are thin and artificially drawn out to fit Gottsched's requirements. The characterisation is far from subtle; Frau Gottsched still uses comic names, *sprechende Namen*, derived from their salient characteristics — Captain Foolhardy, Mrs Honest, Mr Goodfellow, and so on. She is caught between older and newer, more subtly characterised types of comedy. Where she succeeds is in particular scenes, where the dialogue can be very funny indeed, and in the occasional creation of characters who go beyond the conventional. She has a particular talent for the comedy of accumulation. In *Die ungleiche Heirath,* the tired and hungry cousin of the head of the family of impoverished aristocrats has to listen to an endless description of each section of the family's grotesque coat of arms: eleven silver piglets' heads on a blue background; a purple toad on a variagated gold background; six bars on a red background. And the whole is held up by a pair of bears' tails:

Herr v. Wildholz:
> *Nun! das bekenne ich! Ich habe immer nicht gewußt, was ich aus den zwey braunen Dingern habe machen sollen, die an Ihren Kutschen neben dem Wapen angeklecket sind. Sind das Bärenschwänze? Ich dachte es waren Eichhörnchen.*

Herr v. Ahnenstolz:
> *Ja, Bärenschwänze! leibhaftige Bärenschwänze!*

Herr v. Wildholz:
> *Ich dachte ein Schildhalter müßte Hände, oder Tatzen, oder Pfoten, oder Klauen haben, wie die wilden Männer, die Adler, die Löwen, die Bären, die Tyger: daß aber auch ein Bärenschwanz einen Schild halten könne; soviel Unsinn hätte ich der Wapenkunst nicht zugetraut.*

Herr v. Ahnenstolz:
> *Nun! zu Heinrich des Voglers Zeiten konnten die Bärenschwänze das.*

Herr v. Wildholz:
> *Aber hatten die Bären zu Heinrich des Voglers Zeiten, auch Schwänze?*

Herr v. Ahnenstolz:

Warum nicht? Wo es geflügelte Löwen, und zweyköpfigte Adler giebt, da kann es auch wohl Bärenschwänze geben.

(Herr v. Wildholz:

Well, fancy that. I never knew what to make of those two brown things daubed next to the coat of arms on your coaches. So those are bears' tails? I thought they were squirrels.

Herr v. Ahnenstolz:

Yes indeed, actual bears' tails!

Herr v. Wildholz:

I thought to hold up a shield you had to have hands or paws or claws, like wild men or eagles or lions or bears or tigers. But a shield held up by bears' tails - I would not have thought even heraldry quite that ridiculous.

Herr v. Ahnenstolz:

Well, in Henry the Fowler's day bears' tails could do that.

Herr v. Wildholz:

But did bears actually have tails in Henry the Fowler's day?

Herr v. Ahnenstolz:

Why not? If there are lions with wings and two-headed eagles there can be bears' tails too.)[11]

Facsimile of original title page from Die Pietisterey im Fischbein-Rocke. *Ed. Wolfgang Martens (Stuttgart: Reclam, 1968).*

Probably the most successful comedy of Frau Gottsched (which sadly not only was never performed but was actually banned in some German states) was a translation/adaptation, *Die Pietisterey im Fischbeinrocke; Oder die Doctormäßige Frau* (*Pietist Zeal in a Whalebone Corset or The Academic Woman*). The original was Bougeant's *La femme docteur ou la Théologie tombée en Quenouille*, a satire on Jansenism written by a Jesuit. Gottsched recommended the play to his bride-to-be in 1732 and she wrote back to say that she saw many similarities between the Jansenists and the Pietists, who were particularly influential in her native Danzig. Her adaptation appeared anonymously in 1736 and caused quite a furore. In fact, the substitution of Pietists for Jansenists works very well, even though purists might object that the religious language of Frau Gottsched's characters is drawn more from German mysticism, as found in Jakob Böhme, than from German Pietism. Nevertheless, she makes a very funny original scene of the disputation of the women about the exact meaning of being born again. Each gives a complicated and highly obscure mystical definition and claims it is totally clear and obvious, while the others set about being deliberately obtuse. What is historically authentic about the scene is that women were in fact prominent in Pietist conventicles and were given virtually equal status with men as spiritual teachers.[12] Frau Gottsched presents them as pretentious and dogmatic: one of the dogmatic women, Frau Glaubeleichtin (Mrs Gullible), is trying to marry off her daughter (in the absence of her husband) to the cousin of one of the leading male Pietists, instead of to the man to whom she has been willingly betrothed for some time. The outcome is predictable: the leading male Pietist is revealed to be trying to trick the Glaubeleichts out of their property, and the timely return of Herr Glaubeleicht (who does not deserve the name 'gullible') rescues the situation and

11. My translation from *Die Deutsche Schaubühne*, 4 (facsimile of the 1743 edition) (Stuttgart, 1972). *Die ungleiche Heirath*, p.78

12. See R. Critchfield, 'Beyond Luise Gottsched's *Die Pietisterey im Fischbein-Rocke oder die Doctormäßige Frau*', in *Jahrbuch für Internationale Germanistik* 17/2 (1985), pp.112-120

corrects his foolish wife. The play has a strikingly successful comic character in the person of Frau Ehrlichin (Mrs Honest), who comes to complain that the Pietist Magister Scheinfromm (Master Sanctimonious) has been trying to seduce her daughter while preparing her for confirmation. She speaks in dialect, which marks her out socially from the other characters, but she is not presented purely as a figure of fun as a result. Her speech fixes her socially and gives comic vividness to what she says, but she is far from stupid and not characterised condescendingly.

The negative portrayal of the female Pietists in the play has raised for some the question of Frau Gottsched's attitude to learned women in general.[13] It is difficult to detect any proto-feminist consciousness on her part, even though she was regarded as the most learned woman in Germany and told so by the Empress Maria Theresa when the Gottscheds were received in Vienna. Frau Gottsched's characters tend to fall into the categories of the silly and the sensible. Men and women are represented in both categories, an indication that Frau Gottsched took the demands of the drama in question and her husband's concern for popular enlightenment, the triumph of good sense over foolishness, as her guide. Her plays are essentially conservative. They ridicule folly, as in the case of the commoner who is prepared to squander his freedom and his fortune on the stupid aristocrats in *Die ungleiche Heirath*. The satire does not suggest any essential disapproval of the social order but of the folly of seeking advantage from social climbing. While something of an emerging self-confidence on the part of the educated and enlightened German bourgeoisie finds expression in Frau Gottsched's work, she does not challenge the status quo.

Frau Gottsched suffered within her own lifetime as a result of the controversies surrounding her husband's work and attitudes. Gottsched's quarrel with the Swiss critics Bodmer and Breitinger began in the 1740s. Later Lessing became his most devastating critic and guaranteed that Gottsched's reputation would never recover. Despite the many absurdities in Gottsched's approach to literature, this dismissal of him is unjust and Frau Gottsched's reputation has suffered by association with it. Though she wore herself out fulfilling the tasks he laid upon her, her efforts guaranteed that there were actable comedies, both original and in translation, for the German theatre in the coming decades, and if Lessing could complain that he found her *Hausfranzösinn* tasteless when he was resident critic at the Hamburg National Theatre, it should be remembered that he was writing in 1767. In other words the play, written in such a modest spirit, had been part of the repertoire for over twenty years.[14]

13. See, for example, Critchfield (note 12) and R. H. Sanders, '"Ein kleiner Umweg". *Das literarische Schaffen der Luise Gottsched'*, in *Die Frau von der Reformation bis zur Romantik. Die Situation der Frau vor dem Hintergrund der Literatur- und Sozialgeschichte*, ed. B. Becker-Cantarino (Bonn, 1980), pp.170-94.

14. Since I wrote this article an English translation of Frau Gottsched's comedies has been published: *Luise Adelgunde Gottsched, Pietism in Petticoats and Other Comedies*. Translated, and with an Introduction, by T. Keith and J. R. Russell (Columbia, South Carolina: 1994).

Shadow Playwrights of Weimar: Berta Lask, Ilse Langner, Marieluise Fleißer.

Agnès Cardinal

Agnès Cardinal is Honorary Research Fellow at the University of Kent at Canterbury.

1. Agitprop: (agitation + propaganda) a type of popular theatre, first developed in revolutionary Russia, with the sole aim of raising class consciousness and proletarian solidarity.

Nowadays, a casual reference to women in the theatre of Weimar Germany tends to evoke nothing more serious than an image of the prancing Liza Minnelli in *Cabaret*, the film adaptation of Christopher Isherwood's *Goodbye to Berlin*, or the husky voices of Marlene Dietrich and Lotte Lenya intoning Brechtian lyrics from Weill's *Threepenny Opera*. Such is the popular residue of a period in European cultural history during which radical departures in German theatre influenced drama worldwide. Earlier in the century, Naturalism and Expressionism had introduced audiences to subject matter and modes of expression previously considered unsuitable for the stage. Politics, sex and the role of women had become standard themes in European drama by the time Bertolt Brecht, Ernst Toller and Erwin Piscator began to revolutionise dramaturgy on the Berlin stage of the 1920s.

While it is true that in the theatres of the Weimar Republic women continued to be prominent as interpreters, as actresses and as singers, this was also a period when, for the first time in the history of German theatre, plays written by women began to have real impact. *Die Wupper*, Else Lasker-Schüler's avant-garde play of 1909, which elicited consternation upon its first performance in 1919, sparked lively and interesting debates upon its second *mise en scène* in Berlin in 1927. The plays of Berta Lask, Ilse Langner and Marieluise Fleißer (all performed in the late 1920s), however, triggered a public response so hostile as to blight entirely their authors' subsequent careers.

That this should be so might not seem all that surprising in the case of Berta Lask, who had joined the Communist Party in 1923. In that year she wrote a dramatic poem in memory of Rosa Luxemburg and Karl Liebknecht entitled *Die Toten rufen (The Dead are Calling)*. In true agitprop[1] fashion it was performed by one of the many *proletarische Sprechchöre* (proletarian speaking choirs) which issued from revolutionary circles all over Germany. The performance was so successful that it had to be repeated over thirty times at venues all over Berlin. Two years later, Erwin Piscator scored a similar success with a workers'

Berta Lask

[Reproduced from Meyers Neus Lexikon, vol.8 (Leipzig, 1974) p.377. (Allgemeiner Deutscher Nachrichtendienst)]

theatre production of Lask's *Die Befreiung (Liberation)*, a dramatic poem about German and Russian women turning to the socialist cause after the Great War. Lask's greatest success came with *Thomas Münzer* (sic), a play commissioned by the Communist Party to celebrate the 400th anniversary of the German peasant revolt led by rebel Thomas Müntzer in 1525. In Eisleben at Whitsun 1925, the play was put on in the open air as a four-hour spectacular, with hundreds of actors and extras. At least three thousand people watched, and were so enthusiastic that the police, under orders to close down the event, did not dare move in. Lask's triumph in Eisleben established her as one of the outstanding revolutionary writers of the period, and her future as a writer of political plays seemed assured. Indeed, in the wake of her success, the workers of the Leuna chemical plant near Eisleben asked her to write a play in the same vein, this time about the failed workers' revolt at the plant four years earlier. Meanwhile, however, Lask had been blacklisted by the authorities, who regarded her activities as dangerously subversive. From now on, her texts were banned, productions of her plays were closed down and at one point she was even threatened with a charge of high treason. By the time she had finished writing *Leuna 1921. Drama der Tatsachen (Leuna 1921. Drama Based on Fact)* towards the end of l926, no-one was willing to risk its production, although, on occasion, extracts were read out at private political meetings. Thus *Leuna 1921*, arguably Lask's best play, was never publicly performed.

As its sub-title states, *Leuna 1921* is a '*Drama der Tatsachen*'. It was Lask's intention to depict an actual event as objectively as possible. In order to procure accurate data of the rebellion at Leuna of March 1921, she spent a good part of the year 1926 travelling through the Mansfeld region, interviewing participants and eye-witnesses and taking copious notes about how people spoke when they remembered what had happened. The opening stage directions ask for screenings of authentic film footage of the Leuna workers, as well as slide projections of the factory's characteristically shaped chimneys belching out their smoke. In making use of such newly available technology, Lask had clearly been influenced by Erwin Piscator, who had begun his pioneering experiments with film and slide projections a few months before.[2] *Leuna 1921,* however, breaks new ground in the successful dramatisation of a complex historical occurrence which had taken place in the very recent past. In its painstaking attention to factual detail and its honest attempt at objectivity, *Leuna 1921* is one of the earliest examples of genuine documentary drama in Germany this century.

Lask completed *Leuna 1921* a few months before Ernst Toller put the finishing touches to *Hoppla, Wir leben! (Hoppla, We are Alive!)* in 1927, the famous play with which Piscator was to open his own theatre to spectacular acclaim later that year. Written almost concurrently, the two plays share some striking similarities. Both are concerned with the portrayal of social injustice and the systems of power which blight the lives of ordinary individuals in contemporary Germany. Both begin with a prologue presenting a

2. cf. E. Piscator's revue, *Trotz Alledem! (Despite All!)* of 1925 and his production of A. Paquet's *Sturmflut (Tidal Wave)* of 1926.

hero's return to his community after years of incarceration. In *Hoppla, Wir leben!* Karl Thomas, a young revolutionary, is released from a mental asylum where he has spent eight years after losing his reason as a result of a last minute reprieve from a death sentence. In *Leuna 1921* the central figure *Heizer* (the stoker) comes out of prison, where he has languished for five years for his part in the Leuna revolt of 1921. As each hero meets his old comrades, he realises that his suffering has been entirely in vain. Nothing has changed: corruption, injustice and exploitation are as rife as ever. However, the similarities between the two plays end here. With Toller, the prologue takes the form of a flash-back to a group of condemned prisoners in a cell in 1919, while the subsequent main action homes in on present-day Germany; that is, to the events of 1927. In contrast, Lask situates her prologue in the present, while the actual play unfolds as a flash-back to the events of 1921.

Thus, whereas Toller's play deals with the present, *Leuna 1921* is in essence a historical reconstruction. Moreover, *Hoppla!* focuses on the fate of a single, well-defined hero, Karl Thomas, whose life ends in absurdity and existential despair. In contrast *Leuna 1921*'s central figure, the allegorical *Heizer*, is subsumed into the general fate of the rebel group to which he belongs. The audience is encouraged to understand the workers' defeat as a temporary setback within the wider perspective of the universal socialist advance. The twenty-nine scenes of *Leuna 1921* offer a panoramic view of a society divided into two opposing camps; the workers and the bourgeois. While the latter are portrayed as manipulating every instrument of power, the workers' cause is fatally weakened through lack of a coherent plan, through internal squabbling, and through betrayal by the fearful, the indifferent, and by spies, all failing in their loyalty for their own personal reasons. One of the last scenes of *Leuna 1921* shows our group of workers in a prison cell, brutally tortured, preparing to face death.

The prison cell is also the last setting in Toller's play. Karl Thomas, falsely accused of murder, hangs himself. As the light goes out, other prisoners are left to despair. In *Leuna 1921* however, the final gruesome tableau suddenly opens onto the defiant singing of the *Internationale*, followed by an Epilogue in which unidentified workers sing a kind of 'Ode to the Revolution'. Both plays deal with virtually identical material, yet they are worlds apart in message and outlook. *Hoppla, Wir leben!* is an angry statement of human despair. *Leuna 1921*, on the other hand, despite its sombre subject matter, never relinquishes its optimistic socialist stance. It is, in its essence, a didactic exercise which seeks to analyse past mistakes in order to draw lessons for the revolutionary struggle ahead.

It is not altogether surprising that contemporary critics, from both sides of the political divide, received *Leuna 1921* with a distinct lack of enthusiasm. The famous liberal critic of the Weimar period, Alfred Kerr, complained — with some justification — that what he hoped to see in contemporary drama was *'nicht nur Stücke mit guter Tendenz, sondern gute Tendenzstücke'* ('not simply plays with admirable tendencies but admirable tendentious plays').[3] In the Communist

3. F.N. Mennemeier *Modernes Deutsches Drama 1. Kritiken und Charakteristiken. Band 1: 1910-1933* (Munich: Fink, 1973), p. 216.

camp on the other hand, Lask's candid analysis of the shortcomings of the revolutionary *Märzstürme* (*March Storms*) of 1921 was uncomfortably at odds with the heroic history of the Communist advance which was being promoted at the time. All in all, *Leuna 1921* ended up by pleasing nobody, not even those who came to read it in postwar East Germany. One reason for this may be the fact that the play contains frequent and powerfully expressed references to the blight of industrial pollution. In the play the workers of Leuna complain bitterly about the fact that they are forced to produce nothing but *'Dung und Gift'* ('dung and poison') which, while keeping the management's balance sheets healthy, pollute not just the workforce but the world itself. This was not a message which would appeal to incumbent Communist governments of later decades. After *Leuna 1921*, Lask's star began to fade, and in the 1930s she published no more than a handful of strongly propagandist stories. After a brief spell in prison in 1933, the year Hitler came to power, she fled to the Soviet Union, where she remained until her return in 1953 to East Berlin at the age of seventy-five.

Unlike Berta Lask, whose creative *élan* faded as the century wore on, Ilse Langner remained a steady chronicler of the political and cultural turbulence experienced by Germans, from her playwright's debut in 1929 to her death in 1987 at the age of eighty-eight. Although often political, her large and varied *oeuvre* is not determined by any particular ideology, but rather by themes which explore aspects of the rights and roles of women in a society on the brink of disintegration. Her very first play *Frau Emma kämpft im Hinterland* (*Emma's Struggle on the Home Front*) deals with a German woman's experience during the Great War. The very first anti-war play written by a German woman, it created a great stir when it was performed in Berlin's *Theater unter den Linden* in 1929. Centre stage here is not the soldier in a trench but a prototype 'Mother Courage' called Emma Müller, who, with her husband away at the front, is left in sole charge of her household and her child. As conditions deteriorate and

Ilse Langner
(Photo from Ernst Johann (ed.), *Ilse Langner, Mein Thema und Mein Echo*, Darmstadt, p.73)

starvation threatens the civilian population, Emma and the women around her learn to think and fend for themselves. It is a process in which, one by one, old codes and values begin to lose their significance. Patriarchal notions such as patriotism, loyalty to the Kaiser, and, indeed, loyalty to absent husbands, are replaced by the overriding priorities of survival and the care of children. When her small daughter falls ill through malnutrition, Emma coerces her odious, black-marketing lodger into having sex in return for butter, bacon and sausages with which to cook a meal to save the child.

It is in such scenes, where the reinterpretation of gender roles assumes grotesque dimensions, that Langner's play becomes truly memorable. Indeed, the whole play is a study of the options facing women *in extremis*. When Emma becomes pregnant she reluctantly decides to have an abortion. Her maid, on the other hand, consorts with the same lodger for the sole purpose of getting a child who will give her life meaning and stability. Another character, Lotte, an officer's daughter, takes up prostitution because she is quite simply tired of being hungry. It is not difficult to understand why audiences found Langner's play shocking. Here, the war seems to be raging not so much between Germany and its foreign enemies as between German women and their men. Of crucial importance is the final scene when Emma's husband returns from the front. Expecting a hero's welcome, he is completely dumbfounded when a furious Emma berates him for having abandoned his family for four years:

> *Männer seid Ihr? Ihr stürzt Euch in den Krieg wie in einen Rausch und vergeßt alles andere darüber. Uns hier im Hinterland habt Ihr vergessen, wir konnten in Hunger und Kummer und Dreck verrecken! — Ihr seid in Euren Maulwurfsgräben nicht aufgewacht!*[4]

> (Call yourself men? You rush off to war as if out on a drunken spree, letting everything else go hang. You never gave a thought to us here behind the front: for all you care, we might have perished of hunger, worry and filth! — You never once came to your senses, down there, in your moles' burrows!)

Thus she shouts, while her husband vainly seeks to justify himself with speeches about patriotic duty and the hardships of military life. He wants nothing more than to pick up life where he left it four years earlier. Deeply hurt by her anger and upset by her new independence, he watches his wife donning her tramdriver's uniform, ready to go off to work: '*Und wer räumt die Stube auf, und wer kocht mein Essen?*' ('And who will now clean the place and get my dinner ready?'), he complains. Eventually, the two reach a compromise: Emma can keep her job as long as she sees to it that her husband's dinner will always be warm and waiting when he gets home. Thus the play ends on a happy though, by today's standards, hardly uplifting note. Even so, the producer decided to omit this last scene from the performance of 1929: while he could expect audiences to go along with Emma's moral transgressions, and even her hostility to the men at war, the scene where she defies her husband was deemed too explosive. In the end the play was performed to considerable

4. I. Langner, *Frau Emma kämpft im Hinterland. Chronik in drei Akten* (Berlin: 1930. Printed as manuscript by Fischer). New edition: (Darmstadt: Hessische Landes- und Hochschulbibliothek, 1979), p.86.

critical acclaim. Alfred Kerr praised it as a moving and thought-provoking piece; but he clearly spoke for many when taking umbrage at Langner's suggestion that the women's war effort was in any way comparable to that of the men. All in all, the play earned Langner fame and ridicule in equal measure; she was known henceforth as a rabid feminist and nicknamed '*Penthesilea Langnerin*' after the man-eating warrior queen of the Amazons. It took fifty-five years before the play saw the stage again.[5] Langner confronted the charge of feminist intransigence in a subsequent play entitled *Die Amazonen*. Scheduled for 1933, the production was shut down by the authorities during rehearsals. She spent much of the 1930s on extended journeys to the Far East, and all her work was subjected to censorship until 1945. To this day very few of Langner's thirty-three plays have been performed: they remain forgotten even in Germany, where her name is absent from every recent survey of modern literature.

Only in the last decade or so have German critics begun to ask why it is that the plays of Ilse Langner, and especially *Frau Emma kämpft im Hinterland*, have received so little attention, whereas those of her contemporary Marieluise Fleißer have entered the German literary canon. As hard-hitting statements about the correlations of sex and power, Langner's *Frau Emma* (1929) and Fleißer's *Pioniere in Ingolstadt* (1928) would offer great scope for comparative analysis. The apparent arbitrariness with which some works are remembered and others forgotten remains a constant enigma in literary research. In the case of Marieluise Fleißer, the success of her plays today must, at least to some degree, be understood in terms of a surge of feminist interest in the psychology of her relationship with Bertolt Brecht.

5. The play saw a new production in Pforzheim in 1984.

That said, there can be no doubt that Fleißer's two powerful plays of the 1920s are fascinating by any standard. Two years younger than Ilse Langner, Marieluise Fleißer was just twenty-three when she wrote *Die Fußwaschung (The Washing of Feet)* in 1924. She was born in the Bavarian town of Ingolstadt, which she describes as the 'blackest' of Catholic towns in Germany. The play is a harrowing psychological study of teenage life in just such a place. It was the product of what she herself called 'a collision' between her upbringing in a Catholic convent and the dual influence of her mentor, the playwright Lion Feuchtwanger, and the writings of the outrageous young Brecht. Her play focuses on the relationship of Olga, a pregnant schoolgirl, with the ungainly boy Roelle, who foists himself upon her with threats after her boyfriend has abandoned her. Six short scenes

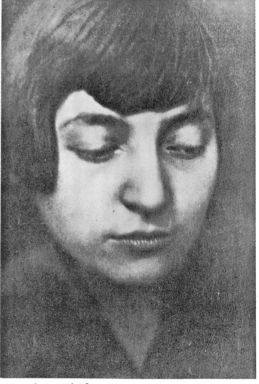

Marieluise Fleißer
(Suhrkamp Verlag, Frankfurt a.M.)

evince veritable miasmas of small-town claustrophobia. Here nothing comes to pass without the knowledge and judgement of the entire community. The play portrays frustration and a repression so intense and all-encompassing that violence is apt to erupt at any time. Roelle, for one, is expelled from school for sticking pins into the eyes of a dog, and is, in turn, subjected to torture at the hands of altar-boys, school-mates, psychiatrists, and even his mother. In a language which continually veers between everyday speech and the rhetoric of Catholicism, the young protagonists struggle with each other as they negotiate the contradictory impulses of wanting freedom and needing to belong. The play has a strong metaphysical dimension in that Olga and Roelle take on the stature of a latter-day Virgin and Christ: as victims, they are at once banal and transfigured.

When Fleißer showed *Die Fußwaschung* to Lion Feuchtwanger he was sufficiently impressed to recommend it to Brecht, who, in 1926, passed it on to Moriz Seeler for a single matinée production at the *Junge Bühne*, the young writers' stage, of the *Deutsches Theater* in Berlin. Brecht went along to help with the rehearsals and liberally crossed out anything in the handwritten text he deemed unsuitable. Seeler, in turn, decided to change the title of the play to *Fegefeuer in Ingolstadt* (*Purgatory in Ingolstadt*), and only thought fit to ask Fleißer for permission to do so later on. Yet it was a crucial decision in so far as Fleißer's name was henceforth indelibly linked in the public mind with that of her hometown.

The success of *Fegefeuer in Ingolstadt* owed not a little to the fact that the two great critics and rivals of the time, Alfred Kerr and Herbert Ihering, for once agreed in their praise of the play. All the same, Kerr could not refrain from speculating as to the extent of Brecht's participation in this creditable effort by *'die tapfere Fleißerin - wenn sie exisitiert'* ('the trusty *Fleißerin* — if, indeed, she exists at all'[6] — for apparently Kerr found it hard to believe that a woman could be such a powerful writer. All the same, Fleißer had begun to make a name for herself as a female avant-garde playwright worthy of note.

It cannot however be disputed that in Fleißer's next play the influence of Brecht was paramount. By now Fleißer had fallen completely and irrevocably under the great man's spell. The idea for her *Pioniere in Ingolstadt* was born on one of her visits to Brecht in Augsburg. Out on a stroll with Brecht, she told him about the stir which the arrival of a group of army pontoon builders had caused among the girls of sleepy Ingolstadt. Brecht immediately gave her the blue-print for a play on the subject:

> [...]*das Stück muß keine richtige Handlung haben, es muß zusammengebastelt sein* [...] *Es muß ein Vater und ein Sohn hinein* [...] *Die Soldaten müssen mit den Mädchen spazierengehen; ein Feldwebel muß sie schikanieren*[7]
>
> [...] the piece must not have continuing action. It must be thrown together in loosely connected scenes [...] There must be a father and a son [...] The soldiers go for strolls with the girls; they must be seen to suffer chicanery at the hands of their sergeant)

6. G. Rühle (ed.), *Materialien zum Leben und Werk der Marieluise Fleißer*, (Frankfurt a.M.: 1973), p.416 and p.37.
7. M. Fleißer, *Gesammelte Werke*, Vol I (Frankfurt a. M.: Suhrkamp, 1972), p.442.

From the outset Fleißer was uneasy about writing the play, since she knew nothing at all about military life, and felt that it really ought to be written by a man. The fact that she at once began to work on it can only be interpreted as a gesture to gain favour with Brecht. The resulting play was first performed in Dresden in 1928 to moderate acclaim. In essence it is a study of the difference in attitudes to sex between men and women and of the brutalising effect of army life on young men. In its original form the play comprised twelve short and, for the most part, interchangeable scenes on the general theme of 'girl meets soldier'. After its *première* in Dresden, Brecht arranged for the play to be transferred to Berlin and, anonymously taking control of the production, set out to transform it into an exercise in audience provocation. Fleißer, who was in any case already diffident about the play and even at the best of times worked slowly and instinctively, felt totally unable to intervene, let alone contest the many changes Brecht made during rehearsals. For instance, he wanted to include a scene in which schoolboys discuss aspects of female anatomy; and he rearranged the stage so that an exchange on venereal disease should take place amid large and looming tombstones. The heroine's defloration, originally off stage, was now given overt treatment by being enacted on stage inside a suggestively rocking wooden box.[8] All these changes were introduced at a hectic pace and things were still being rearranged as the curtain went up. Fleißer was by now so angry and disillusioned that a break with Brecht was inevitable.[9] Yet nothing had prepared her for the storm that was about to break. In the audience at the first showing of *Pioniere in Ingolstadt*, Police-Chief Weiss of Berlin, himself a former sapper, saw the play as an insult to military honour. When he complained, the offending scenes were cut from the production, whereupon the play, as Brecht had rightly calculated, became a huge success as Berliners flocked to see what it was all about.

Although Fleißer had become famous, a virulent press campaign was now unleashed against the play and its author. Right-wing nationalists voiced their outrage at this negative portrayal of the German military by a woman who had no right to meddle in what was clearly a male domain. Others complained about this monstrous young woman who seemed to revel in the coarsest indecencies. The most wounding reaction for Fleißer came from the burghers of Ingolstadt who, although few of them could have actually seen the play, considered themselves personally insulted by it. There began a hate campaign during which the burgher-master of Ingolstadt filed charges against Fleißer for libel and her father forbade her to visit the family home. Within a few days, Fleißer came down with a nervous fever; later that year she became engaged to a right-wing journalist. Although some of her best writing was yet to be done, her public career was now over. In the 1930s her books ended up on Hitler's bonfires and she spent the next two decades in her 'banal exile' in Ingolstadt, married to a tobacconist.

Today Marieluise Fleißer is best known for her short stories. Her plays are occasionally performed in Germany, and while not

8. M. McGowan, *Marieluise Fleißer*, 'Beck'sche Reihe Autorenbücher' (Munich: 1987), pp.52–53.

9. cf. 'Avantgarde. Erzählungen' in *Gesammelte Werke*, Vol. III, pp.117–168.

exactly eliciting rapturous receptions, usually gain a certain *succès d'estime*. And rightly so, for both *Fegefeuer in Ingolstadt* and *Pioniere in Ingolstadt* are significant prototypes within twentieth-century experimental drama. As such they have played a crucial role in the shaping of modern dramatic theory, even if only by briefly supplying Brecht with a safe testing-ground on which to work out his ideas about the *Volksstück* and 'epic theatre'. It seems to me time to retrieve from the shadows the legacy of playwrights who for one reason or another are in danger of disappearing altogether from public awareness. It is of course too late to establish with certainty, for example, whether Brecht's Mother Courage is indeed a direct descendant of Langner's Frau Emma, or to what extent Toller and Lask were aware of the convergences of their material as they wrote in 1926. Research on the work of Ilse Langner has barely begun. As for Berta Lask, German history has all but buried her. Yet it is as well to remember that, for a short while in the 1920s, her plays commanded the kind of mass audiences that Brecht could only theorise about.

Bibliography

Primary Texts

M. Fleißer, *Gesammelte Werke*, I (Frankfurt a. M.: Suhrkamp, 1972).

B. Lask, *Leuna 1921 - Drama der Tatsachen* (Berlin: Internationaler Arbeiter-Verlag, 1927).

E. Toller *Hoppla, Wir leben! Ein Vorspiel in fünf Akten* (Potsdam: 1927); *Hoppla! Such is Life!* tr. by H. Ould in *Seven Plays* (New York: Liveright, 1934).

I. Langner, *Frau Emma kämpft im Hinterland. Chronik in drei Akten* (Berlin: 1930. Printed as manuscript by Fischer). New edition: (Darmstadt: Hessische Landes- und Hochschulbibliothek, 1979).

Secondary Material

K. Grünberg, 'Berta Lask. Fünfundsiebzig Jahre alt' in *Neue Deutsche Literatur*, 2 (1954), pp. 167–169.

L. Hoffmann & D. Hoffmann-Ostwald, *Deutsches Arbeitertheater 1918-1933*, I & II (Munich: Verlag Rogner & Bernhard, 1973).

K. Kändler, *Drama und Klassenkampf* (Berlin: Aufbau, 1970), pp.129-142.

M. McGowan, *Marieluise Fleißer*, 'Beck'sche Reihe Autorenbücher' (Munich: 1987).

F.N. Mennemeier *Modernes Deutsches Drama 1. Kritiken und Charakteristiken. Band 1: 1910-1933* (Munich: Fink, 1973), pp.212-215.

U. Münchow, 'Berta Lask, Hermynia Zur Mühlen und Maria Leitner' in *Deutsche Literatur von Frauen*, II, ed. G. Brinker-Gabler, (Munich: Beck, 1988), pp.262-268.

F. Rothe, 'Lask, Fuchs und Gotsche — drei literarische Vorlagen für "Märzstürme 1921"' in *Sozialistische Zeitschrift für Kunst und Gesellschaft, Politik und Theater - Märzstürme 1921*, W. Schwiedrzik (Berlin: 1972), pp.15–17.

G. Rühle (ed.), *Materialien zum Leben und Werk der Marieluise Fleißer*, (Frankfurt a.M.: 1973).

I. Stephan, 'Weiblicher Heroismus: Zu zwei Dramen von Ilse Langner' in *Frauenliteratur ohne Tradition? Neun Autorinnenporträts*, I. Stephan, R. Venske, S. Weigel (eds.), (Frankfurt a.M.: Fischer, 1987), pp.159-189.

H.-G. Thalheim et al. (eds.), *Geschichte der deutschen Literatur*, X (Berlin: Volk und Wissen Volkseigener Verlag, 1978), pp.270-271 and 319-320.

E. Tunner, 'Aufbruch' in *Deutsche Literatur von Frauen*, II, G. Brinker-Gabler (ed.) (Munich: Beck, 1988), p.408.

Women Playwrights on the London Stage; 1918-1968
Maggie Gale

Maggie Gale is Lecturer in Drama and Theatre Arts at the University of Birmingham.

Because so little has been written on women's theatre history, all kinds of misconceptions continue to flourish [...] part of the problem derives from the emphasis of so much theatre scholarship on text based theatre. This is to some extent understandable since theatre is ephemeral and the written playscript is all that materially remains after the performance has ended. But to focus on the written text creates an imbalance. [1]

The first post-1968 publications documenting the placement of women in theatre were largely written by feminist theatre historians who in the main were writing about feminist theatre. They were limited to the documentation and analysis of certain periods in history; the Edwardian and the so-called 'rebirth of the women's theatre', which itself came out of the rebirth of the women's movement in the late 1960s with, until recently, only a limited regard toward the women playwrights of the Restoration period. This imbalance is being rectified by more recent research into the history of female performers, directors, managers and administrators. However, in terms of textual analysis, just as prioritising text over performance produces imbalance, so too does the study of only certain *kinds* of texts which fit into pre-defined analytical frameworks.

This analytical framework has included analysis of theatre produced by women, whether textual or not, but one of the key qualifications for inclusion was evidence of a deliberate connection between aesthetics and feminism. Many have neglected to acknowledge the multitude of work produced by women who did not fit into the frame, namely those who were involved in the production and creation of theatre between 1918 and the late 1960s.

During the 1920s and 1930s organised political feminism was far less visible; struggles to improve the position of women within society continued, but less publicly. Organisations continued to argue and work around specific issues, such as contraception and child-care, and within working-class organisations feminism still found a presence. But theatre work controlled by women, linking feminism and aesthetics, ceased to command its own space. There were a number of women who were very active within the Unity Theatre movement [...] and there was the occasional play about the 'women question' — equal rights for women, equal educational opportunities, abortion. But it was only well after the Second World War that feminism and theatre came together; this time in a greatly changed social and political situation in which radical post-war changes to the family had produced intense and contradictory pressures on women. [2]

1. S. Bassnett, 'Struggling with the Past; women's theatre in search of a history'. *New Theatre Quarterly*, V,18, (May 1989), p.108. (CUP).
2. M. Wandor, *Carry On Understudies* (Routledge, 1986), pp.3-4.

There has been a general failure to recognise a notion of 'feminisms'; a multitude of political and ideological positions concerned with the social, economic and historic placement of women. A statement that women lived under contradictory pressure only after the Second World War fails to acknowledge the 'real' social and economic position of women during the years which spanned the end of the First World War and the mid 1960s. The validation of a Marxist materialist feminism over bourgeois feminism, or vice versa, can lead to the misrepresentation of contexts for women's struggle for equal status.

Writers such as Dale Spender, Joanna Alberti, Shari Benstock and Virginia Smyers have documented some of the less visible work carried out by 'feminist' women during the middle period of the twentieth century. Certainly, the struggle for women's equality did not have the same momentum, form or focus as it had once had during the era of the Suffragette. Yet the struggle continued over disparate but connected issues, many of which failed to attract the same *public* attention as had the fight to establish votes for women. This is not to prioritise the private over the public, but rather to point to its possible equivalent significance.

The Actresses Franchise League (the A.F.L.) is seen as an example of a feminist theatre valid in its equivalent ideology and practice to that of the feminist theatre of the late 1960s, but rarely are any crossover points with the theatre which followed the brief history of the Actresses Franchise League acknowledged. Auriol Lee, for example, acted for Edith Craig's Pioneer Players whose work was connected to the A.F.L., and went on to become one of the most prolific commercial directors of the 1930s, directing most of Van Druten's London productions up until her early death in 1942.

Some feminist historians have perhaps unintentionally misrepresented particular periods of history in order to stress the importance of what is being examined in their own particular highlighted period of interest. Consequently, we find statements like the following;

> During the period from 1660 to 1720, over sixty plays by women were produced on the London stage — more than from 1920–1980.[3]

This information is misleading and incorrect. It signifies a particular period of history as being an exception in terms of women's creativity and theatre. To some extent, the statement validates cultural assumptions about the invisibility of women in theatre history. One group of writers are foregrounded at the cost of another, so women remain on the margins and their creative presence is the exception rather than the rule.

> False categorising (which) ranges from the mythologising assumptions that prevent clear seeing [...] to biased misjudgment, to plain lying; at its worst its the deliberate renaming of phenomena so as to change their significance. [4]

3. N. Cotton, *Women Playwrights in England 1363–1750*. (London: A.U.P., 1980), pp.16-21.
4. J. Russ, *How To Suppress Women's Writing* (The Women's Press,1983), p.43.

Helen Keyssar reveals the inherent contradictions in a closed model for analysis when she writes:

> Between 1919 and 1960, the most persistent gesture towards feminism in drama was a focus on female characters and the particular obstacles these characters encountered because they were women.[5]

In terms of bringing woman's experience as written by woman into the public arena of theatre, the persistent gesture of these female playwrights should not be so easily dismissed. Readings of the plays reveal unquestionable connections between their work as artists and their socio-economic position as women. Keyssar differentiates between post-suffrage playwrights and those of the period after the late 1960s:

> As the contemporary playwright Honor Moore has remarked, 'whether or not they identify themselves as feminists, there are now playwrights whose art is related to their condition as women.' The plays created in the context of that recognition do not just mirror social change but assert a new aesthetic based on the transformation rather than the recognition of persons.[6]

What is being identified as a persistent gesture for one generation becomes aligned with a semi-radical position for another. Not all contemporary women playwrights are concerned with new aesthetics or transformation as opposed to recognition of persons. In a 'theatre society' where there exists little public recognition of female person as written by woman, the making public of *recognition* is integral to any future process of *transformation*.

Women Playwrights 1918-1968

Between 1914 and 1968, the context for British theatre and society was influenced by two World Wars, The General Strike, fluctuations in economic stability, changes in the proportional ownership of theatres, changes in taste, and the introduction of state funding for theatre amongst other things. Women were moved *en masse* from the home to the public workforce during the First World War, back into the home, back into the public workforce, then back to home and duty once more. The period also hosts developments in a virtual solidifying of definitions of socially acceptable and biologically imperative 'female' and 'feminine' behaviour.

During the 1920s, 1930s and, to an extent, the 1940s, the British stage was made up of commercial theatres, repertory theatres, small club theatres — such as The Everyman, The Gate, The Embassy — and subscription club theatre groups which hired or ran venues such as The Savoy and The Kingsway. Although there were exceptions, such as Clemence Dane's *A Bill of Divorcement*[7] and Dodie Smith's *Autumn Crocus*[8], many of the dramatic successes on the West End stage started life in these 'other theatres' which by today's standards were run by professionals but, more often than not, on an unpaid basis. Similarly, plays are not likely to be taken into a commercial theatre today unless the management can be

5. H. Keyssar, *Feminist Theatre* (Macmillan, 1986), p.25.
6. Ibid. p.1.
7. C. Dane, *A Bill of Divorcement* (Heinemann, 1961).
8. C.L. Anthony, *Autumn Crocus* (Pan Books, 1967).

persuaded that there will be a financial gain. New writers reached a larger audience via the then equivalent of our 'fringe theatres'. Writers like Susan Glaspell, Paul Claudel, actors such as Sybil Thorndike, Gielgud and Gwen Ffrancon-John achieved their first British 'successes' through this fringe system.

A number of women playwrights wrote mainly one-act plays, which fitted perfectly into a one-night programme of three 'one-acters' by new writers, or were used as 'curtain-raisers', performed immediately before a main production. Many of them also concentrated on plays written for children which again have been historically devalued. Neither of the latter two have any real economic value for theatre producers in a commercially oriented theatre. It is also important to note that there were often many more actresses looking for employment than actors. Press-cuttings and comments made by women working during this period do show that gender prejudice still existed and some women directors, such as Edith Craig, felt that a lack of available work was due almost entirely to the division of employment opportunities being based on gender bias.

There were in fact considerably more than sixty plays by women produced on the London stage between 1918 and 1968 alone, the majority of which were concerned in some way with inequality between the sexes, the inherent contradictions in the social and moral expectations of women, and representations of women in history.

Playwrights such as Gertrude Jennings, Gwen John, Clemence Dane, Gordon Daviot, Margaret Kennedy, Aimée Stuart, Dodie Smith, Esther McCracken, Joan Temple, Enid Bagnold and Bridget Boland, to name a few, were 'jobbing' playwrights. Many of them were also journalists and later wrote film scripts: they earned significantly more acclaim and money from their theatre writing than their future counterparts .

A significant number of these plays either had all women casts, or made women central to the action and narrative as protagonist or antagonist. These playwrights came up against the same constraints and bias as women during the late 1960s, a few even gave themselves androgynous names like C.L. Anthony (Dodie Smith) and Gordon Daviot (Josephine Tey). One of the most interesting socio-political facts about the early playwrights of the period is that a large proportion began their careers as actresses and (it is argued), by finding it hard to get good parts, ended up writing them themselves.

It is, however, impossible to categorise the work of the women playwrights of the period in terms of a notion of shared 'sisterhood'; although where they are mentioned in historical writings by critics they are marginalised into chapters such as 'Our Women Dramatists'[9] and likened to the 'feline tortoise-shell cat'[10]. Many of their plays are as 'well-made', and possibly bourgeois, as any of those written by their male counterparts. Equally, some of them, such as Susan Glaspell, Brigitte Boland and Anne Jellicoe, experimented with form and style of writing, although experimentation with form was rare until the 1950s, and most of the playwrights use the well-

9. E. Short, *Theatrical Cavalcade* (Eyre and Spottiswoode, 1942).

10. L. Hudson, *The Twentieth Century Drama* (Harrap and Co., 1946).

made play, the style of twentieth-century melodrama, and often the 'drawing room' setting. Thus their work cannot truly be seen as homogeneous. However, there are certain clearly identifiable traits of common interest and thematic focus.

The majority of the plays are set in traditionally 'female' spaces; inside the home, in all-female working environments, and so on. Many have either all-female casts, or female characters are in the majority, and the plots are often centred around women's lives and experiences. So during a period when we are led to believe by some theatre historians that there was no 'significant work' being done by women in theatre, there is a visible wealth of playwrighting which not only brings discourse centred on the *private* lives and experiences of women onto the *public* stage, but also creates new employment possibilities for actresses and, strangely (if we are to believe the somewhat neurotic bleatings of a few of the contemporary male drama critics), also brings a new female audience into the theatres. Many of the women dramatists wrote self-consciously about the nature and conditions of women's lives, their place in the economic order and their difficulty, not so much in finding a voice but in finding an acceptable and workable identity.

One prevailing feature of the plays written by women of this period is a desire to explore and indicate the existence of a cultural state of confusion of identity, a mismatching of social and moral expectations and the lived experience of women. Many represent an attempt at analysing the position of women in a social and economic, and therefore power-based, relationship to both men and society.

The Man Who Pays the Piper

G.B.Stern's *The Man Who Pays The Piper* [11] was first performed in London at the St Martin's Theatrein 1931 with a cast that included Diana Wynyard and the young Jessica Tandy. It is a serious attempt to analyse the relationship between gender and socio-economic power. The play only had a short run in the West End, and was criticised by some for being too intellectual and undramatic, yet by others it was acclaimed as her best piece of drama. It is a three-act, 'well-made' play centred around seventeen years in the history of the middle-class Fairley family. The play begins in 1913, and opens with an argument between the key character Daryll and her father. Dr Fairely disapproves of one of her friendships.

> And now since she's stuffed you up with all this fudge about votes for women — Suffragette processions and I don't know what [...] the next thing is I shall have you burning down churches [...] throwing acid into letter boxes. [12]

To which Daryll replies;

> Alexia's wonderful. I can't bear silly little half-witted flappers [...] I wish you'd let me join Alexia's business when I've finished my training [...] what's the use of learning anything. I'll sit at home and be useful and cut bread and butter [...] I want to be independent. [13]

11. G.B. Stern, *The Man Who Pays The Piper* (Samuel French, 1929).
12. Ibid. p. 9.
13. Ibid. pp. 9–10.

Stern opens the play by establishing a differential between three close generations of Edwardian women and their social ambitions, as well as establishing the rule of the patriarch as being reliant on the fact that it is he who holds the economic power.

The audience are then taken forward to 1926; Daryll's father and elder brother have been killed in action and she is now the head of the family. The male characters in the play are shown as being financially inept. Her mother's new husband is a musician without work — Daryll's sister's husband the same. They constantly ask her for financial support as she is now the head of her friend Alexia's business, which has become a large West End concern. The men discuss women and power with such statements as:

> **Ben:** She's not masculine to look at. I can't bear women with gruff voices who cover half the room in a stride.[14]

Daryll herself feels that she cannot get married because she already has such a large family to support. She sees herself as the father of the family:

> [...] in this house [...] there isn't a father [...] not one single father except me [...] Of course I come home and behave abominably [...] It's got into my bones [...] And all the men come to me as man to man and thank me rather resentfully for what I've done [...] I'm not going to wish this on any daughter of mine. [15]

Act Two is full of discussions on economics, gender and power, where Daryll points out that it is the 'man who pays the piper who holds the purse strings that plays the tunes.'[16] Stern presents a vibrant contrast in Daryll's sister, Fay:

> This is 1926, Independence and work and bright young bachelor girls [....] Oh no I'd much rather live at home.[17]

The Act ends when Daryll's mother inherits a fortune from one of her dead husband's patients. At this point, Daryll turns to her long-time fiancé and asks him to

> [...] take me, marry me, smash me, begin me all over again, and make me into the usual sort of wife [...] it's not too late [...] I don't care how you do it [...] but break me.[18]

Act Three is set four years later: Daryll has been married two years, she has given up work and taken on the domestic role; she feels bored and unchallenged. When she discovers that the business that she helped to build up is in a state of collapse Daryll goes against her husband's wishes and decides to go back to work, telling him:

> Oh Rufus [...] you're being quite unendurably silly and such a cave man. This isn't the time to stand with folded arms and a rocky scowl [...] If I hadn't been bored from morning till night do you think I'd have been so wildly frantically glad to get back again [...]back to my business [...] oh to have something to do again [...] something continuous and constructive [...] I'm no good for marriage [...] it's the war, we had to take over then [...] I expect

14. Ibid. pp. 40-41.
15. Ibid. pp. 60-65.
16. Ibid.
17. Ibid. p. 70.
18. Ibid. p. 77.

there's a whole generation of us [...] We're none of us fit for marriage, we fathers of nineteen fourteen [...] I'm a freak. We're all freaks my generation of girls [...][19]

Her husband, who feels that they cannot both work (that is to say, take on a 'masculine' role), offers to become a 'house husband' saying that it is just traditional prejudice which says that men must work and women must weep. Daryll rejects his suggestion as being 'unnatural', and because of this reaction he tells her that she is *perfectly* conventional, *perfectly* feminine and she falls into his arms. There might be the end of the play except that Daryll does go off to 'save' the business and the ending of the play is left open with her leaving saying, 'just this once, we can arrange things differently afterwards'.

Stern's play brings up all kinds of questions about the nature of femininity. Daryll's femininity has been constructed through social and historical imperatives. She represents a whole generation of women who were required to leave their traditional feminine roles behind and take control during the war, and were then literally dropped from the public domain when the war was over. One of the key questions which Daryll asks, and others ask of her, is whether she can be both economically powerful and feminine. She struggles to find an acceptable feminine identity which fits her actual fragmented experience. The discourse of the play is centred around recognition and a need for transformation. Both genders discuss feminine social roles in terms of their social constructedness rather than their biological innateness. Daryll's confusion and fragmented experience of femaleness is seen as a symptom of a political and economic system based on the supply and demand of labour. She is not a victim of patriarchal ideologies as much as capitalism itself.

Contemporary writers of the period, such as Winifred Holtby,[20] were aware that, especially amongst the 'new' philosophies of the sexologists in the 1930s, there was a very strong desire to discredit the notion of 'equality of the sexes'. Simultaneous to praising feminists, Havelock Ellis also felt that, 'the Banner under which they fought, while a wholesome and necessary assertion in the social and political realms, had no biological foundation.' Ellis was greatly alarmed at the idea that women should have the, 'same education as men, the same occupations [...] This idea he described as the source of all that was unbalanced, sometimes a little pathetic and a little absurd in the old women's movement...He wanted women to have independence [...] this was to be achieved through an endorsement of motherhood.'[21]

Stern was concerned that a woman's personal fulfilment cannot be achieved through family or marriage alone; that a woman should have the opportunity for fulfilment in the public as well as the private sphere. The play exposes a desire for emergence, a need to break out of constructed roles into ones created by need and experience.

Women of Twilight

Sylvia Rayman's *Women of Twilight*[22] works on a social-economic rather than a social-psychological level. Rayman is interested in

19. Ibid. pp. 95-98.
20. W. Holtby, *Women in a Changing Civilisation* (Lane & Bodley Head, 1934), p.109.
21. S. Jeffreys, *The Spinster and Her Enemies* (Pandora, 1985), p. 137.
22. S. Rayman, *Women of Twilight* (Evans Bros., 1951).

moving from emergence to exposure. In *Women of Twilight,* Rayman's first play (written while she was working in a London snack bar), there is a deliberate subverting of the image of 'charming English home life'.

Originally staged at The Embassy in 1951, transferring to The Vaudeville and then playing briefly on Broadway, the play was later made into a film . It is a tragic but socially observant tale of the life of single mothers living on the margins of society, in the 'twilight zone.' The action of the play is staged in a semi-basement living room of a large house near London. The room is characterised by neglect and untidiness. Helen Allistair is a widowed middle-class woman who at first glance appears to be a well-meaning philanthropist, providing shelter and childcare for a community of women who have in common the fact that they cannot find homes because they are single mothers, who have to earn their living as well as carry out the job of mothering.

During the first act, we are introduced to some of the women who live in the house. Rosie is an eighteen-year-old 'factory girl', and Laura presents herself proudly, as here, as an unmarried mother:

[…] I don't want no man tied to me […] all I wants is my baby.[23]

Sal is the ex-maid who now looks after the children; she is old and rather slow, hardly featuring in the play until her dramatic revelations in the final act. Vivianne is expecting a child by a man who is on trial for manslaughter, and Christina has just arrived at the house with her very young son. The women are unsettled and unhappy; they are caught in the poverty trap in that their wages only just cover the rent and childcare fees; few of them manage to save any money and the only escape is provided by the hope of either the return of the estranged fathers of their children or through finding another man to marry. It is not long before Vivianne reveals the true nature of Mrs. Allistair's supposed altruism:

[…] I didn't want this baby […] nine out of ten are like Rosie and they're better game for Allistair than the wiser ones. She takes every penny they've got and lets them live in squalor and talks to them like the salvation army […] all her saccharine talk about taking the homeless in off the street and giving them shelter; shelters just about all at three guineas a week with a quid on top if you want her to look after the kid. [24]

The first Act draws to a close when Rosie comes in from a day out with her boyfriend to reveal that she has been told that her child has malnutrition; Helen Allistair's response is:

[…] He may be weak and sickly, but that's the result of generations of squalor and ignorance and unwholesome stock […] some mothers were not in a condition to produce model babies […] healthy trees produce healthy fruit.[25]

The second Act ends when Christina comes back from a week away to find her child on the brink of death. In Act Three Vivianne has a conversation with the old maid, Sal, who tells her:

23. Ibid. p. 14.
24. Ibid. p. 23.
25. Ibid. p. 34.

[...] one day Nellie (Allistair) 'it 'im with a stick and 'e just lay there on the carpet. I wanted to put 'im to bed but Nellie said it weren't no use, 'cos he was dead [...] she says girls like me didn't ought to have babies and if they found out they'd put me in prison.[26]

Vivianne's suspicions are reaffirmed when she is told by Sal that, 'Nellie used to take in babies and the nice ladies who 'adn't any babies of their own would take them away.' Vivianne says:

A lot of things go on that the public don't want to know. So they look the other way — the same as the Welfare people do when they come down here. They're not really fooled by the show you put on for them, but its easier not to look too closely. I've seen so much dirt I'm not squeamish anymore. [27]

One attempted murder later we come to the last scene of the play. The whole of the basement has changed; it is now bright and clean. Christina returns to the house to be told by Allistair that Vivianne has had her child and is unable to see anyone as she is so close to death. Finally, Helen Allistair's evil intent is revealed and her final words are spoken centre stage, just before her arrest:

[...] sluts all of you with your rotten little bastards. I took you off the streets, when decent people wouldn't look at you. God when I think what I've done for you; slaved morning and night. What have I kept for myself since my husband died. I gave up my house to you, and this is how you repay me. You've no gratitude, no loyalty [...] how dare you speak to me, you sanctimonious little bitch.[28]

In her preface, producer Rona Laurie points out how the play 'challenges the social conscience of the audience'.[29] It condemns, through Helen, a bourgeois and Victorian attitude toward the poor and in particularly toward single unmarried mothers. The physical stage space is interior and claustrophobic. Laurie suggests that a small cramped stage can only enhance the mood of the play. Helen Allistair is a product of her own greed and sociopolitical beliefs, left over from the 'days of the Empire'. Her bitterness is taken out via the exploitation of others, usually women of a lower social class, under the guise of philanthropy. As Deidre Beddoe has acknowledged, 'housewife and mothers [...] this single role was presented to women [...] to follow all other alternative roles was presented as wholly undesirable'.[30] What Rayman is clearly expressing in her play is the complete contradiction in women's 'inherent' social roles, in a society that cannot cater ideologically or economically to the requirements of its so-called moral culture.

Both of these writers have much in common with many of the other women playwrights of the fifty year period under discussion. Lib Taylor has recently stated that writers like Agatha Christie were successful in their theatre writing largely because their plays re-affirmed cultural stereotypes[31] and acted as a form of imaginative anaesthetic against the immense social changes that were happening after the Second World War. Yet when we look at a greater selection of plays written by women of the period, very clear patterns of

26. Ibid. p. 78.
27. Ibid. p. 81.
28. Ibid. p. 91.
29. Ibid. pp. 5-7.
30. D. Beddoe, *Back To Home And Duty* (Pandora Press, 1985), p. 137
31. L. Taylor, 'Early Stages; women dramatists 1958-68', in *British And Irish Women Dramatists Since 1958*, T.R. Griffiths & M. Llewellyn Jones (Open University Press, 1993).

dissension become apparent in their choice of focus, both in terms of character and narrative. During the 1950s there were a whole series of texts where the place of motherhood and the role of mother was put into question and challenged. Again, during the early 1930s, where the eugenics movement and the rise of fascism in Europe became important components in a cultural political system where women were being encouraged back into the home and into private domestic roles, there are a number of plays written by women and produced in commercial theatres to acclaim, where the connection between motherhood and femininity were put directly into question.

Writers of the period under discussion, such as G.B. Stern, Susan Glaspell, Gordon Daviot in the 1920s and 1930s, and Margaret Neville, Joan Morgan, Rose Franken, Sylvia Rayman, Aimée Stuart, E.M. Delafield in the 1940s and 1950s, do not often directly refer to specific political events or movements which specifically effect the lives of women. However, an understanding of both the source and effect of new cultural ideologies and sociopolitical movements which were contemporary to their playwrighting careers, is vital to an understanding of what is being foregrounded in their work.

My point is that those of us who are interested in text must allow ourselves to expand our framework of analysis beyond the confines of a *closed* feminist framework. Unless we can do this, then we are refining an already refined version of women's place in theatre history, and negating the possibility of re-discovering an historical continuum of work by women playwrights. When I began my research I was completely unaware of the vast number of plays written by women and produced professionally between 1918 and 1968 in Britain. Obviously, and this could be seen as somewhat subjective, some of the plays are as 'unworthy' as texts as any of those which are both 'unworthy' and written by men. Yet many are valuable, both as indicators of developments in playwrighting by women during a period when there was, superficially, no large and homogeneous political pressure group for them to identify with or against, and as links in a chain of unwritten history. Further links in the chain can be found in plays written by women for the amateur theatre, which thrived in Britain during the inter-war period; but this research is only just beginning.

Thus, from studying the work of women playwrights produced on the British stage between 1918 and 1968, it becomes clear that writing women's work out of theatre history based on an analysis of either its commercial, feminist or contemporary political validity alone invites only marginalisation, ghettoising, and the depleting of the importance and cultural significance of women's creative presence in theatre throughout history. There have been women writing for a multiplicity of theatres throughout this century in Britain, 'writing out the experience of the female into public dramatic fiction'[32] — and faction.

32. L. Walsh Jenkins, 'Locating The Language Of Gender Experience', in *Women and Performance Journal*, II (1984), pp. 5-20.

Women & Theatre in Italy: Natalia Ginzburg, Franca Rame & Dacia Maraini

Sharon Wood

Sharon Wood is Senior Lecturer in Italian at the University of Strathclyde.

In 1954 the American writer and theatre critic Eric Bentley commented that 'Italy, ever as poor in drama as she is rich in theatricality, is finding that a profession of playwrights cannot be legislated into existence even with the help of subsidies.'[1] Bentley was echoing the despair expressed by Luigi Pirandello in *Sei personaggi in cerca d'autore* some thirty years previously: in the absence of good new writing in Italy, what was there for a company to put on if not a translation of a foreign play or something by the incomprehensible Pirandello himself? And forty years on from Bentley's own essay there are those who will say that not much has changed: the theatre in Italy continues to surprise by its failure to foster new writing, and to alarm by its dependence on state subsidy to the point where political allegiance rather than artistic merit stands as guarantor for both jobs and productions. In the arguments about public funding of the arts, Italy in some ways plays the part of the devil's advocate in suggesting that it simply does not work, and there are those who would dearly love to see a temporary moratorium on ill-directed backing, as on yet another production of Pirandello, Goldoni or Shakespeare, or on pieces which could be labelled 'experimental'.[2]

Yet, as Bentley comments, Italy is a country rich in theatricality, the dramatic impulse diverted perhaps from the stage onto the street. Such theatricality was clearly in evidence when feminism in Italy was at its most public: and I would perhaps be better off here speaking not of some putative feminist aesthetic of theatre but of the theatricality of Italian feminism.

Women's marches and demonstrations in the late sixties and seventies were remarkable for their colour, show and vivid representations of women's lives. Judith Malina's accounts of productions put on with Italian women in the mid-seventies by the Living Theatre, based on women's own lives and experiences, underline the point that much grass-roots Italian feminism expressed itself, often for the first time, outside the institutions, outside established genres, outside language even, in forms which were inherently theatrical rather than discursive or even linguistic. She describes a play put on jointly between women of the Living Theatre and the local women of Faenza, 11 November, 1976:

> The Women's Play: at the OMSA factory [...] taking the theme from our discussion: The inability to speak - and even the unwillingness to speak in what Dimitra called 'the male rhetoric'[...] We face the entrance to the workers' cafeteria, standing in a line in which we cannot see one another. At a sound cue we raise our

1. E. Bentley, *Thinking about the Playwright* (Illinois 1986), p.278.
2. G. Anselmi, 'Che cali il sipario', in *Lo stato del teatro*, edited by Renzo Bortolotti, (Bari, 1992).

arms in the Delta symbol of the Feminists: We are silent, a tape speaks for us. It's a tape of Women's stories, complaints, abuses. It speaks alternately of the abuses of daily life, and of the local and dramatically known incidents — of rape, abortion, deaths, lost jobs [...] We try to take a step forward, silently, our symbols over our heads, and we balance slowly and precariously, but we do not speak — cannot, will not, do not speak[...] Tape speaks [...] And then the tape stops and we strain in a chorus of non-verbal sounds, we stretch forward and our mouths move and our faces are contorted with the years of our oppression and we want to speak — but we have no voice [...] As in the common dream.[3]

It is no accident that in Italy a great number of those who have written for the theatre have first established their credentials in other genres.

Of the writers under discussion here, Natalia Ginzburg and Dacia Maraini are known principally as novelists, while Franca Rame made her name primarily as a performer. Ginzburg works within the conventions of mainstream theatre, even while she questions some of its practices. Maraini's more overtly political and politicised theatre takes account both of ideological shifts in the cultural practice of the political left in Italy and of pan-European experiments and developments in dramatic form. Franca Rame incorporates her feminism within a left-wing political stance that meshes closely with, but does not displace, the artistic practice of popular theatre. I would like to relate the very diverse dramatic aesthetic of each writer — working within mainstream, political or popular theatre — to their own reflections on feminism and politics, tracing connections in their work between the aesthetic and the political as they are embodied in dramatic form.

I should say that the involvement of women in Italian theatre has a very long, if obscure, tradition. Women were closely involved with the *Commedia dell'arte* not just as actresses but as *capocomico*, running companies and producing their own material. In his memoirs Goldoni gives due credit — for example — to women such as Isabella Andreini, and Franca Rame traces her own artistic practice back to these women. In more recent times two women have written for the stage, even if their work has been completely sidelined by a very maschilist literary tradition. Caterina and Cecilia Stazzone[4] both wrote for the theatre in Sicily in the late nineteenth century: Annie Vivanti, now seen by many critics as little more than an appendage to her more famous lover Carducci, wrote some powerful pieces for the Milan stage around the First World War, describing polemically the plight of women when a hostile army invades, and raising the uncomfortable call in a rigidly Catholic Italy for ethically sanctioned abortion.[5] I should also say that there has been almost no critical work done on these writers, and it is still difficult even to get hold of texts.

Natalia Ginzburg began writing for the theatre in the 1960s. Like many of her contemporaries, she despaired about the state of Italian theatre: the paucity of new material, the stifling predominance of a few — almost exclusively dead — masters, the ease with which

3. K. Malpide, *Women in Theatre: Compassion and Hope* (New York: 1983), p.216.

4. See, for example, C. Stazzone, *Cinque Commedie* (Siracusa 1989).

5. A. Vivanti, *Gli invasori* (1918).

even poor productions could be given extensive runs and tours if the right backing — meaning the right political contact — was available.

Ginzburg's plays have been strongly criticised by some for having very little about them that is theatrical: indeed, they consist entirely of dialogue, or rather monologue; a narrative in which the speaker recalls his, or more often her, past experience. These are intensely undramatic in the Shavian sense. Ginzburg cannot be placed within the tradition of bourgeois realist theatre or the well-made play; nor does her work directly reflect the avant-garde formal experimentalism taking place in European theatre at the time. One critic has commented on her work, that:

> the most conspicuous characteristic of Ginzburg's theatre is precisely the absence of any kind of action [...] when there is something happening it is secondary, if not fortuitous; what matters is what is said, what matters above all is the selfish silence of the world outside, ready to swallow up and eliminate the voices of the speakers.[6]

To stop speaking is often, for her characters, to recognise the fragility of their own position in the world and to admit the abyss at the heart of their own lives. Language is not used as exchange of information, unless it be to convey a sense of the collapsing world outside, the disintegration of a relationship or the impossibility of dialogue. In this sense perhaps there is some connection between the work of Ginzburg and that of Beckett. Language represents not communication but non-communication: the difficulty of speaking together symbolically represents the difficulty of living together; the profound isolation of the individual.

If Ginzburg's theatre hovers on the edges of 'realism', her relationship to feminism is equally complex. She pleads against the limiting reductiveness of any orthodox ideology of male oppression, even as she recognised it as one mode of inter-gender relationships. While agreeing with all the practical demands of feminists, she finds unacceptable the ideological assumption she sees underpinning second-wave feminism, and a prior assumption that women are simultaneously oppressed and somehow superior beings. She acknowledges the imprint of our sex on our minds and characters, but simultaneously aspires to a transcending of the specifically personal and sexual:

> The difference between men and women is the same difference that exists between the sun and the moon, or between day and night [...] In our best moments, our thought is that neither of woman nor of man. And yet it is equally true that on everything which we think or do there lies the imprint of our individual physiognomy, and if we are women, the female signs of our temperament stamp themselves on our words and actions. But our ultimate aim is to reach a domain where men and women alike can recognise themselves in us, and where our personal physiognomy is forgotten.[7]

Ginzburg does not accept that thought, or art, is gendered. Paradoxically, it is in accepting that she writes like a woman (after several misbegotten attempts to write 'like a man') that Ginzburg

6. E. Clementelli, *Invito alla lettura di Natalia Ginzburg* (Milan 1972), pp.95-96.
7. N. Ginzburg, 'La condizione femminile' in *Vita immaginaria* (Milan 1974).

sees herself writing as a human being.

Ginzburg began writing for the theatre relatively late in her career, and she approaches the theatre very much as she does her much better known stories and novels. Writing remains for her an essentially private act which is then translated into dramatic form. Ginzburg comments particularly on the way in which her female characters are rewritten, re-cast perhaps, in the transition from text to performance.

> I usually imagined my women small, fragile, restless and untidy. But the theatre plays terrible tricks on you. The people putting on the play didn't care a bit if I said I had imagined these women small, and often they chose instead tall, well-built actresses. And sometimes I had poor people in mind, but on the stage we got people with beautiful clothes who looked quite well off. I would protest, but I couldn't fight them. They would say to you that the theatre has its laws. Sometimes these laws are absurd and inexplicable, and they take you miles away from the creature born in your imagination.[8]

Even while she echoes the anxieties of many a writer for the theatre about loss of control over their work, Ginzburg betrays here an essentially idealist, writerly approach that does not see the writer as involved in a joint collaborative effort with director, actor, designer and so on. Ginzburg as 'begetter' of the text, born in her imagination and yet escaping her, can be juxtaposed with the maternal figures she portrays, who must at all costs be eluded, transcended almost, while they attempt to determine meanings which are contrary and inevitably in flux. It is tempting to see this as an unwitting metaphor for Ginzburg as writer for the theatre.

The figure of the mother, already examined in Ginzburg's prose works, is dominant in her theatre, even if she frequently never even appears on stage. In *L'inserzione*, premiered in London in 1965 with Joan Plowright, the lonely and abandoned Teresa and the young student who comes to her flat in response to an advertisement for a lodger find in their mothers an immediate topic of conversation.

In *La porta sbagliata* (1970), the mothers of the troubled couple, Angelica and Stefano, are always on the phone, an invisible but constant presence suggesting a distant hold not yet broken, like an uncut umbilical cord.

In Ginzburg's first real success in the theatre, *Ti ho sposato per allegria* (1964), Giulia and Pietro's recent marriage appears to be a spontaneous and almost unmotivated decision. Their union, not based on traditional bourgeois grounds of social compatibility or economic interest, is examined in the light of the attitudes of their parents; mothers in particular. Pietro's mother is convinced her son has made a ghastly mistake taking in this girl who is poor, unconnected and who shows no due respect. The figure of the mother, as presence or object of conversation, dominates all three acts, and is finally dismissed as the couple resolve to determine their own lives, to make their own decisions: 'At a certain point we have to send them packing, don't you think? We can love them very

8. N. Ginzburg, quoted in A. Bullock, *Natalia Ginzburg* (Oxford, 1992), p.65.

much, but we have to send them packing.'[9]

Ginzburg's main characters are frequently those who do not appear on stage - for whom no actor will get paid. A number of the plays are structured around an absent character, usually male: what happens or is said onstage are ripples or reflections, the flotsam and jetsam of bigger events being played out elsewhere. This dislocation of the dramatic event identifiable in Ginzburg's theatre has led to a comparison with Ionesco, Albee, Pinter and Beckett.

Her work has been defined together with theirs by one strand of theatre criticism as 'il teatro delle chiacciere', the 'theatre of chat', indicating as the critic Pullini puts it 'not so much a defective lack of dramatic action as a deliberate and intentional filling of the scene with lines which appear to wander at random and which in fact are the face of an underlying dramatic substance that barely makes itself felt.'[10]

The distance between the 'teatro delle chiacchiere' and contemporary intellectual and political movements of the late sixties and early seventies was underlined by Pier Paolo Pasolini. His Manifesto for a New Theatre was based less on some dubious notion of committed literature than on his idea of the Teatro di Parola (a Theatre of the Word) which was to be neither the traditional/academic bourgeois theatre of chat nor the avant-garde theatre of the Gesture and the Scream. Theatre, wrote Pasolini, should be a 'debate, an exchange of ideas, literary and political struggle.'[11]

Dacia Maraini was similarly interested in finding a way between more traditional theatrical forms in which language degenerated into empty and meaningless exchange, and extreme forms of modern experimentalism which avoided engagement with language at all.

For Maraini the refusal to acknowledge the primacy of the word in theatre indicated the rejection of thought, a narcissistic pandering to the subconscious:

Theatre has lost the word. It has become deaf and dumb — an angelic, paralysing deafness. A devastating, violent muteness. Theatre now expresses itself through more sublime images which are abstract and diabolical: more and more suggestive, but less and less significant.

The sleep of reason generates monsters: white, libidinous larvae, cackling birds which rise up out of the darkness as Goya's painting, while man sleeps [...]

Our cellars pulsate with these larvae which have emerged from the great night of our dreams. The unconscious clothes itself in paper, paints its face and walks barefoot on the boards of our underground stages.

But the unconscious is indiscriminate and mixes what is sublime with what is stupid and vulgar, and has no desire to distinguish between them. The unconscious excludes choice. It comes out as a spontaneous gushing and slides heavily over things.[12]

We have here an implicit statement of the dilemma of Italian theatre,

9. N. Ginzburg, *Ti ho sposato per allegria e altre commedie* (Milan, 1968).
10. G. Pullini, *Tra esistenza e coscienza: Narrativa e teatro del 1900* (Milan, 1986), p.274. Alberto Moravia comments on the *teatro delle chiacchiere* that 'the chatter certainly alludes to something serious, tragic even: but this something is not revealed, and remains wrapped in a mysterious darkness. As a result we have a maximum of conventionality, absurdity, fragmentoriness — in other words, chatter — and at the same time the tormenting, mystical feeling that cannot be the whole world, that it is impossible not to go behind the chatter and discover something higher, deeper, complex: in other words, the dramatic'. A. Moravia, 'La chiacchiera a teatro' in *Nuovi Argomenti*, no. 5 (1967), p.10.
11. P. P. Pasolini, 'Manifesto per un nuovo teatro' in *Nuovi Argomenti*, no.7 (1968), p.24.
12. D. Maraini, *Fare teatro* (Milan, 1974), p.66.

KING ALFRED'S COLLEGE
LIBRARY

torn between those who approach it as literature and those who approach it as performers and directors. Directors will accuse the writers of being bourgeois: writers will accuse performers — as Pasolini accused Dario Fo — of being anti-intellectual. For Maraini the absence of writers in the theatre leads to excessive formalism, abstraction, and a distancing of the theatre from the real needs and concerns of ordinary Italians. The separation of the functions of writer and director, fused together in figures such as Pirandello and Lorca, and the cult and power of artistic and theatre directors, left little space for the autonomous writer.

Unlike Ginzburg, Maraini was — indeed, is — actively involved in the business of setting up and running theatre companies, and her theatre has consistently taken into account both her feminism and her politics. She began writing for the theatre in the late sixties, together with Moravia, Siciliano, Gadda and a number of others.

Her company *La compagnia blu*, and later *Teatroggi,* were set up under the aegis of the Communist party and atttempted to establish themselves in the Roman suburb of Centocelle with the given cultural aim of *decentramento*, decanting theatre from established theatrical spaces inhabited only by the élite.

Later Maraini set up the very successful theatre workshop, the *Teatro della Maddalena*, run by and for women writers and including seminars and workshops for a number of women at the beginning of their writing careers.[13]

Relations between innovatory theatrical practitioners and the Communist Party were never particularly smooth. Dario Fo, for example, clashed with the Party over their reformist tendencies. Opening up the theatrical process to a new public risked greater consequences than perhaps the PCI was prepared to contemplate. Observers such as Marco de Marinis have commented on the way in which the Party took fright once its theoretical pronouncements on the need for self-managment, alternative touring circuits and decentralisation began to be put into practice.[14]

Maraini explores the dialectic of the problematic conundrum of theatre and politics, the confluence of artistic and political practice, and the innovatory possibilities of dramatic form.

> (The)irritation of politics made theatre and at the same time the need to make political theatre. Our love of form is polluted by the doubt that this love is a privilege reserved for those on the side of power. There is a cruel feeling about the impotence of the word and simultaneously the certainty that only the word can say with clarity and poetry what we want.

> There is the refusal of the theatre of shadows, the theatre of the irrational, the theatre of terrorism, in other words the avant-garde, and at the same time the awareness that the best of our theatre today comes from the most formalistic directors, the ones most dedicated to shadows and aestheticism.

> There is our love for collective work and at the same time horror at the approximations and fudges which pass for the democratic

13. Teatro della Maddalena finally closed in 1990. Maraini blames consistent lack of public funding for its demise.
14. Marco de Marinis, *Il nuovo teatro 1947-1970* (Milan, 1987), p.345.

process, the clashes and hostility which are held in check only by ideological necessity.[15]

One of Maraini's most striking plays is *I sogni di Clitennestra*, (*The dreams of Clytemnestra*) written in 1973.[16]

In this reinterpretation of Aeschylus, Clytemnestra is both the character from Aeschylus and a housewife from a town somewhere north of Florence whose husband has emigrated to America in search of work; Aegistheus is a good-for-nothing, incapable of holding down a job yet living off his lover; Orestes is the avenging, tormented son and a *gastarbeiter* in Germany. Iphigenia is both killed as propitiatory sacrifice and married off to settle a debt, subsequently dying in childbirth.

Maraini does rather more than turn tragedy into soap opera. The merging of lines from Aeschylus with a more modern idiom (the shading in and out of Aeschylus' story with the experiences of an ordinary Italian in the 1970s) lead to some startling and sometimes moving juxtapositions, and some intensely dramatic moments when what is dreamt overlays — or undermines — what actually occurs. The death of Agamemnon takes place as he lies in bed with his American mistress Cassandra: she believes the murder is only a terrible dream, and sings him a lullaby to soothe him. In the modern version of the story, Clytemnestra's belief that she has murdered her faithless man reveals itself to be a delusion as she is threatened with electric shock treatment in the asylum.

Clytemnestra's 'madness', her unconscious, her dreams, her sexuality, which she refuses to suppress during the long absence of her husband, represent a disestablishment of patriarchal order, an inversion of roles. This is why Clytemnestra must die at the hands of her son, her throat cut at a family dinner while all the other characters calmly proceed with their meal. The central clash in the play is between Clytemnestra and her daughter Electra, and constitutes a hard-hitting debate about the allegiances of women that take the form of a power struggle between patriarchy and matriarchy. Agamemnon states the fundamentally Western philosophical claim of patriarchy to Electra: 'I gave birth to you with my imagination. Your mother contributed her guts. I gave the truth.'

Mother and daughter are as clay within the patriarchal hands, to be given shape, form and life by him alone. Clytemnestra makes her own plea for solidarity:

> You and me, face to face. I'm the same as you. A woman who stinks of onions and the washing. Just like you. But you don't look at me. You don't see me. You think of him, over the sea. Your eyes are heavy with black light. You, my daughter, a woman like me, instead of being on my side you live only for him, you lick the ground where he walks, you keep his bed warm, you are his spy, his guard-dog. (p.68)

In this play Maraini makes a sustained attack on the family as institution, as purveyor of a petit-bourgeois hypocritical morality,

15. D. Maraini, *Fare teatro* (see n.12), pp.5-6.
16. D. Maraini, *I sogni di Clitennestra* in *I sogni di Clitennestra e altre commedie* (Milan, 1974).

as a perversion of eroticism. Yet just as *I sogni di Clitennestra* is more than tragedy in modern dress, so it is also more than a feminist tract informed by a healthy dose of psychoanalysis. The real polemic of the piece emerges at the end of the play when the Furies — both of the ancients and three wizened old prostitutes — appear to Clytemnestra in her cell. The matriarchy, powerful force of the unconscious and the hidden power of femininity that they represent, have been tamed, defused, have sold out. 'It is science which has changed us', they say:

> We have been converted by democratic reasoning [...] we have been tamed for the sake of good relations between men and women. We who used to defend the reasons of women bearing epidemics into the midst of men, now we do penance licking the floor of the house of God [...] We have been tied up, cut into pieces. We have lost our fury like an ancient illness [...] Now we are happy. We are putrid with happiness. Livid with pleasure.

Franca Rame.   (Max Whitaker, supplied by Methuen)

Maria Stuarda (*Mary Stuart*), written in 1978, sheds more light on Maraini's sexual politics. Readers of the Scottish writer Liz Lochhead's play *Mary Queen of Scots Got Her Head Chopped Off* (1986) may be interested to see how close the two writers are in their solution to specific problems of staging. The central relationship in Maraini's play is that between Mary and Elizabeth, each of whom act — almost literally — as a mirror to the other. The fascination of intra-female relationships leads to the dramatic casting solution of doubling; having the actress playing Elizabeth also playing the part of Mary's servant, and vice versa.

Maraini states repeatedly her refusal to put her politics above her art. This most politicised and consistently feminist of writers still recognises the supremacy of art over propaganda, of creativity over political rhetoric, the greater power of the imagination than of the ideological tract. Readers of her plays might question how far she succeeds in this. The writer/performer who clearly does succeed in keeping politics subservient to drama is Franca Rame, longtime companion and partner of Dario Fo. The attribution of authorship to Franca Rame (even of her feminist monologues) is clearly problematic, given the working relationship with Dario Fo and the finalisation of texts not on the page but on the stage, in rehearsal. Fo and Rame established their own theatre cooperative, *La Comune*, which was to dispense with traditional hierarchical working practices and create collective decision-making and planning while playing to an alternative circuit.

Like Maraini, they discovered the project to be a utopian one, but they shared with the radical intellectual Left the need to break with traditional forms and traditional spaces. Also like Maraini, Fo and Rame identified with the non-sectarian Left, critical of the Communist party, which was perceived to be too rigidly authoritarian, hierarchical, as well as patriarchal; too locked in rigid ideology, too inimical to culture, as well as too timid for revolution. Their political stance led to serious consequences: in 1973 Rame was kidnapped and raped by a fascist gang.

Rame is by no means a radical feminist, and is critical of what she calls brutal, hard-line feminism: 'I am in complete agreement with those women who are struggling for liberation, once and for all, from those senseless inhibitions which have been inculcated into us over the years. But I would always, even when dropping my knickers, like to achieve that with a minimum of style.'[17] She differs from an orthodox feminist interpretation of Euripides' *Alcestis*, for example, preferring to see in the play not an exhortation of women's selflessness and self-sacrifice but a condemnation of a collective failure of nerve. The jointly authored *Coppia apperta* turns out to be a heartfelt defence of the family as an institution of strict monogamy. She will have nothing to do with feminism in its more theatrical form: 'On the subject of feminism', she continues, 'things seem to have taken a turn for the better, now that certain forms of hysterical extremism have been done away with. Many of the women who, in the early days of passion and fervour, celebrated their emancipation with witches' dances leading up to the final rite (thankfully merely allusive) of castration of the male, have now returned to humdrum normality as home-owners, happy mothers and smiling brides.'

Laughter with anger, *riso con rabbia*, is Rame's guiding principle. Humour and satire are the essential elements of Fo and Rame's style of theatre. As long as satire exists there remains the possibility of democratic politics, and it is satire which becomes the great debunker of the phallocratic myth.

> You have to agree that from the very dawn of time, men have always given the most grandiloquent of names to their organ [...] but that word organ always sidetracks me. It makes me think of St Peter's. Anyway, the anatomical details of the male organ have always rejoiced in high-sounding names. Phallus! what a ring it has to it [...] Gland! This could be the name of some exotic flower. 'Here, darling, take this sweet scented bouquet of glands and clasp it to your breast.' There could be a Sophoclean epic constructed with this terminology[...]

17. F. Rame in *Dario Fo, Tricks of the Trade* (London, 1991). Translated by J. Farrell.

Nothing of the sort could be attempted with the terminology foisted on us women [...] 'Vagina'! The best you could do with a vagina is slip on it. The word uterus is even nastier. It sounds like an insult, or an offensive weapon [...] And I don't want to hear about the 'vulva'! [...] Peruvian ant-eater. In any case, it is unquestionably poisonous [...] These words are only fit for horror stories:

The first prize must go to another term, one that I can hardly bring myself to utter - orgasm! It is a word addressed almost exclusively to women. Men experience pleasure, but women orgasm. The very sound is enough to make the hairs stand up on the back of your neck. It summons up monsters [...] Can you see the headlines in the morning paper: 'Giant orgasm escapes from city zoo!' 'Nun assaulted by mad orgasm on run from American circus'.[18]

Rame is only being half ironic here. Yet her range as an actress enables her to embody not only the farcical absurdity of much of women's lives, but also its deeper pathos and even tragedy. Her dramatic and multi-voiced monologues range over issues of rape, terrorism, work and housework, childcare and the Church. Like Maraini she turned also to the classics, and in her interpretion of *Medea* made common cause with Clytemnestra in decrying the abandonment of the older woman for the younger. While Pasolini's wonderful film has Medea suggest the primitive, the rawly emotional, the rural — the unruly unconscious even — defeated by the thrusting, urban ambitious Jason, Rame's *Medea* posits the more banal but equally tragic situation of the woman who, having lost her looks, loses her claim on society and on her man. 'Everyone's embarrassed by a woman who's surplus to requirements.'[19] The murder of her children becomes for Medea a conscious act not of revenge but of breaking the patriarchal law which demands that women sacrifice themselves to their children.

While Ginzburg is less concerned than either Maraini or Franca Rame to tackle directly political issues in her plays, all three writers use their writing to turn the spotlight on contemporary society, and more specifically on relationships between the sexes. There is obviously — and happily — no such thing as a feminist dramatic aesthetic. The very diversity of women's approaches to the theatrical representation of their experience reflects and underlines the dramatic multiformity of that experience. Art will not be subject to ideology, and it is in claiming the independence of aesthetics from politics that these women writers paradoxically enact the liberation that they seek.

18. Ibid., pp.105-6.
19. D. Fo and F. Rame, *Medea* in *A Woman Alone and Other Plays*, ed. Stuart Hood (London, 1991), p.64.

intellect
EUROPEAN STUDIES SERIES

Theatre and Europe (1957 to 1992)
Christopher J McCullough and Leslie du S Read
A study of the relationship of theatre history to the development of both the European Union and the wider continent. A volume in three parts, the first two focus on those aspects of theatre that sought to shape, define, challenge or celebrate the ideals of a united Europe. The third considers the implications for theatre arising from the collapse of the Berlin Wall. A series of essays is included on representative figures of the period both within European Union, and at its margins, such as Václav Havel and Heinrich Müller.
£14.95, paperback   ISBN 1 871516 82 X   *Available 1996*

Children and Propaganda
Judith K Proud
A consideration of how the messages received by youth have been subverted to promote the ideologies of political regimes at key points in the 20th Century. The author examines the consequences for societies when children become adults, and how education should be considered in this light.
£14.95, paperback   ISBN 1 871516 83 8   *Available May 1995*

Humour and History
Presented by Keith Cameron
An insight into the role that humour has played in various European cultures, encompassing satire, irony and ridicule through the centuries. This centres on an examination of people's attitude to laughter and the use of it to influence public opinion.
£14.95 paperback   ISBN 1-871516-80-3   *Available now*

Regionalism in Europe
Edited by Peter Wagstaff
A study of regional aspirations in the Europe of the 1990s in the context of the EU. This volume offers an examination of the relationship between state and region, centre and periphery, capital and province.
£14.95, paperback   ISBN 1-871516-84-6   *Available now*

EUROPA

An International Journal of Language, Art and Culture

Editor: Keith Cameron (Exeter)

Editorial Board

Christopher Cairns (Westminster)

James Coleman (Portsmouth)

Alain Croix (Rennes II, France)

Eleanor Dand (Bristol)

Robert Di Clerico (W Virginia, USA)

John Fletcher (E. Anglia)

Margaret-Ann Hutton (Durham)

Alex Longhurst (Exeter)

Judith Proud (Swansea)

Keith Reader (Kingston)

Maya Slater (London)

Tim Unwin (W. Australia)

Peter Wagstaff (Bath)

Alan Williams (Exeter)

Joanna Woodall (Courtauld Institute)

Gar Yates (Exeter)

Notes for Contributors

Articles will be welcome on any aspect of European art, culture, history, literature, etc. for consideration by the Editorial Board for inclusion in a future issue of *Europa*. Suggestions from interested parties or potential guest editors for complete issues are also invited.

Submissions should be between 2500 and 6000 words in length, with black and white illustrations where possible, although no financial contribution can be made towards payment for the use of copyright material.

All contributions should be presented as hard copy as well as in the form of an ASCII file format on a 3.5inch disk. *Europa* is prepared using Apple Macintosh computers and ideally disks should be supplied in that form, although any IBM-compatible 3.5inch disk is acceptable.

All correspondence regarding contributions to *Europa* should be sent to:

Dr Keith Cameron,
Queen's Building, The University,
EXETER, EX4 4QH, U.K.
E/mail: K.C.Cameron@uk.ac.exeter
Fax: 44 (0) 392 264377

Europa is published four times per year by Intellect Books, Suite 2, 108-110 London Road, Oxford OX3 9AW, UK. The current subscription rates are £18 (personal) and £54 (institutional). A postage charge of £6.00 is made for subscriptions outside of Europe.

Enquiries and bookings for advertising should be addressed to the Journals Manager, Intellect Books, Suite 2, 108-110 London Road, Oxford OX3 9AW, UK.

© 1995 Intellect Ltd. Authorisation to photocopy items for internal or personal use or the internal or personal use of specific clients is granted by Intellect Ltd for libraries and other users registered with the Copyright Licensing Agency (CLA) in the UK or the Copyright Clearance Center (CCC) Transactional Reporting Service in the USA provided that the base fee is paid directly to the relevant organisation.

KING ALFRED'S COLLEGE
LIBRARY